The Victoria Cross

in 100

OBJECTS

The Victoria Cross
in 100
OBJECTS

The Story of the Britain's Highest Award For Valour

Brian Best

FRONTLINE
BOOKS

The Victoria Cross in 100 Objects

This edition published in 2021 by Frontline Books,
An imprint of Pen & Sword Books Ltd,
Yorkshire - Philadelphia

ISBN 978 1 52673 076 3

Pen & Sword Books Limited incorporates the imprints of Atlas, Archaeology, Aviation, Discovery, Family History, Fiction, History, Maritime, Military, Military Classics, Politics, Select, Transport, True Crime, Air World, Frontline Publishing, Leo Cooper, Remember When, Seaforth Publishing, The Praetorian Press, Wharncliffe Local History, Wharncliffe Transport, Wharncliffe True Crime and White Owl.

PEN & SWORD BOOKS LTD
47 Church Street, Barnsley, South Yorkshire, S70 2AS, England
E-mail: enquiries@pen-and-sword.co.uk
Website: www.pen-and-sword.co.uk

Or
PEN AND SWORD BOOKS
1950 Lawrence Rd, Havertown, PA 19083, USA
E-mail: Uspen-and-sword@casematepublishers.com

For more information on our books, please visit
www.frontline-books.com, email info@frontline-books.com
or write to us at the above address.

Printed and bound in India by Replika Press Pvt. Ltd.

Typeset in 10/14pt Adobe Caslon by SJmagic DESIGN SERVICES, India.

Contents

The Idea for a Democratic Award

There are several people who could legitimately claim to have first suggested the awarding of an all-ranks gallantry medal. One to have a strong claim was *The Times* special correspondent, William Howard Russell, who accompanied the Army to the Crimea. He was to witness the three major battles of September to November 1854; Alma, Balaclava and Inkerman. He was given free rein by his editor, John Delane, and filled the paper with his eyewitness accounts. As early as 30 October 1854, he received a generous letter from *The Times*' proprietor, John Walter, acknowledging the emphasis on highlighting the plight of the ordinary soldier: '… the credit due of having added another laurel to the crown of the "Fourth Estate" by the fidelity and zeal with which you have "reported", even on the field of battle, and evidently at considerable peril, the glorious achievements of our troops; while you have certainly earned their gratitude by making known their needless hardships.'

Duke of Newcastle 5th Duke (1811-1864) det.

Russell, W.H. by Matthew Brady.

Russell learned from conversations in the camps of the bravery displayed by the British soldier. He wrote suggesting the Queen might create an order of merit or valour and that it should bear her name. Russell's reports almost certainly influenced the Bath MP, Captain George Scobell, to raise the question in the House of Commons on 19 December 1854 requesting the bestowal of an 'Order of Merit to every grade and individual'.

This suggestion was taken up by the Duke of Newcastle-under-Lyme, the Secretary of State for War. He was to be severely castigated in his handling of the British contribution to the war against Russia and subsequently sacked. He did, however, support the idea of a new democratic award when he wrote to Prince Albert: 'I hope I am not taking too great a liberty if I ask Your Royal Highness's opinion upon the other suggestion, the institution of a new decoration to be confined to the Army and Navy, but open to all ranks of either service.'

Once the concept of new gallantry award took root, the royal couple actively embraced their role in its development. It was a tangible means for Queen Victoria to be seen as the head of her Army and Navy.

Design of the Victoria Cross

What came first in the manufacture of the Victoria Cross; the design or the material? The answer must be the design, which had to be approved by Queen Victoria. The firm appointed to design and make the new gallantry award was the jeweller Messrs Hancock who, in a short time, received the royal appointment with virtually all the crowned heads of Europe. The concept of a democratic award for outstanding bravery irrespective of rank had been in discussion during much of 1855. The involvement of the royal couple, particularly Prince Albert, meant that there was pressure on the Government to follow through with a commitment to produce a single gallantry award.

There seems little doubt that the designer of the Cross was a young man named Henry Hugh Armstead (1828–1905), who worked briefly at Hancock's before going on to find wider fame as a co-designer, sculptor and illustrator. He notably worked on the Palace of Westminster and the Albert Memorial, and became a Royal Academician. As the designer of the Victoria Cross, he has been almost completely overlooked.

Based on the design for the Peninsular Gold Cross, the first copy submitted to Victoria and Albert was rejected. In a letter dated 5 February 1856, to Lord Panmure, the Secretary of State

VC Protype.

Armstead, Henry Hugh 1879 VC Designer

for War, she wrote: 'The Cross looks very well in form, but the metal is ugly; it is copper and not bronze and will look very heavy on a red coat with the Crimean Ribbon. Bronze is, properly speaking, gun-metal; this has a rich colour and is very hard; copper would wear very ill and would soon look like an old penny.'

Despite bronze being so hard that it broke the steel dies, the alternative was to die-cast, a much more wasteful process leaving a rough specimen that necessitated finishing by hand chasing and varnishing. The next sample was in bronze with a plain suspender bar connecting to the Cross with small round links. This was also rejected and a suspender bar with laurel spray and a V-link emphasising Victoria's hand in the design was finally approved.

It was clear that Messrs Hancock, having accepted this project, had to adapt from die-stamping to die-casting the VC. They used time-consuming skilled workers to transform the rough casting into the fine and detailed features of this royal award. On 4 March 1856, Hancocks was instructed to prepare 106 specimens ready for early 1857 with the names of the recipients published in *The London Gazette*.

The VC Cannon

Although no official documents can be found, it is almost certain that the bronze for the new Victoria Crosses appropriately came from the Russian cannon captured at Sebastopol. This is confirmed by a sentence in *The Times* report of 2 March 1857 that the new Crosses were 'formed from the cannon captured from the Russians' and again mentioned in the 1862 advertisements made by Hancocks to the effect that the VC and 'the miniature Victoria Cross, made from the Gun Metal taken at Sebastopol, can only be obtained at C.F. Hancock's'. Certainly, there were enough cannon lying at the dock at the Woolwich Arsenal, which prompted the War Office to ask towns throughout Great Britain to collect a trophy for display as a war memorial in their squares and parks. Many took up the offer and although some since have been reduced to scrap, there are still plenty on display around the country.

The first Victoria Crosses, which lasted for fifty-eight years, were made from the bronze of a single Russian cannon until the supply ran out in 1914. Although there was literally tons of Russian ordnance lying in public places around the country and, indeed in the Woolwich Arsenal store at the Rotunda, the subsequent Crosses have been made from the bronze of Chinese cannon. In what might be an apocryphal account, the order went down the chain of command to some fitters tasked with sawing off the cascabels (attachment points) from Russian cannon. Entering the crowded gun store, the fitters took the line of least resistance and selected the nearest guns, which turned out to be two cannon captured in 1860 at the Taku Forts at the mouth of the Peiho River in the Second China War. In John Glanfield's definitive article on the subject in *The Journal of the Victoria Cross Society* (March 2006), he writes of the completely different make-up of the bronze between the Russian and Chinese cannon.

VC Cannon at Woolwich.

VC Cannon captued at Sebastopol.

VC Ingot.

Both guns are approximately 18-pounders of mid-nineteenth-century manufacture and are 9ft 4in and 10ft long respectively. The missing cascabels at the rear of each gun indicate the region from which the VC metal was taken. Today the guns clumsily sit on Russian Venglov-pattern iron carriages, an arrangement that would have proved lethal if fired. Originally they would have been fitted to teak siege-gun carriages with heavy studded wheels. For decades the two cannon stood outside the Rotunda and later on the parade ground at the Woolwich Barracks before finally being cleaned up and put on display in the Firepower Museum at the Woolwich Arsenal.

The surviving bronze ingot is regarded as the most precious lump of metal in the world and is kept safety locked up in the Defence Storage Distribution Centre at Donnington, Shropshire, and rarely put on public display.

The Warrant

Having agreed that a new gallantry award was to be established, the incoming Liberal Secretary of State for War, Lord Panmure, sought information on how other prominent military countries worded their regulations under which similar awards were given. The Government looked at Spain and Russia before settling on Austria's Order of Maria Theresa, which closely followed the warrant of the new British award. A draft was sent to the Queen, who was happy for Albert to make any adjustments, omissions and inclusions that he thought would cover all eventualities. Naturally this was not to be, and a series of appendices followed soon after. In fact, the Victoria Cross has evolved throughout its 165-year life, with mostly additions to its many warrants. These included European members of the Indian Army (Indian Mutiny), Colonial soldiers (throughout Victoria's reign) and Native members of the Indian Army (belatedly in 1912).

Under pressure from family members, Edward VII agreed that a batch of six historic posthumous awards should be granted, which was announced in *The London Gazette* on 15 January 1907. For such a milestone, there was no warrant issued. During the First World War, when some 295 posthumous awards were made, it was generally accepted without opposition. It was finally made official in Appendix XII dated 22 May 1920, when Clause Four was published stating that the Cross may be awarded posthumously.

There were some short-lived appendices, including Appendix VI, which extended the Victoria Cross to cases of conspicuous courage and bravery displayed under circumstances of danger *but not before the enemy*, something the civil servants viewed as an inconvenient secret. It was only used on two occasions and quietly dropped. Another anomaly was Appendix X, which extended eligibility for the Victoria Cross to the Indian Ecclesiastical Establishments in 1881. This was instigated at the insistence of General Frederick Roberts to enable his chaplain, James Adams, to receive the Victoria Cross for saving the lives of a couple of troopers whose mounts were floundering in a ditch within range of the enemy. Unsurprisingly, this has only been used once.

Queen Victoria was particularly defensive of the warrant, which she saw as Albert's definitive work and should not be touched. The extension of her Empire forced the changes and today's warrant is as good as a set of rules that has taken more than a century and a half to perfect.

Prince Albert.

App.ᵈ Victoria

Victoria by the Grace of God of the United Kingdom of Great Britain and Ireland Queen Defender of the Faith &c: To all to whom these Presents shall come Greeting. *Whereas* We taking into Our Royal consideration that there exists no means of adequately rewarding the individual gallant services either of Officers of the lower grades in Our Naval and Military Service or of Warrant and Petty Officers Seamen and Marines in Our Navy and Non-commissioned Officers and Soldiers in Our Army. *And Whereas* the third Class of Our Most Honorable Order of the Bath is limited except in very rare cases to the higher ranks of both Services and the granting of Medals both in Our Navy and Army is only awarded for long service or meritorious conduct, rather than for bravery in Action or distinction before an enemy, such cases alone excepted while a general Medal is granted for a particular Action or Campaign or a Clasp added to the Medal for some special engagement, in both of which cases all share equally in the boon and those who by their valour have particularly signalised themselves remain undistinguished from their comrades. *Now* for the purpose of attaining an end so desirable as that of rewarding individual instances of merit and valour We have instituted and created and by these Presents for Us, Our Heirs and Successors institute and create a new Naval and Military Decoration, which We are desirous should be highly prized and eagerly sought after by the Officers and Men of Our Naval and Military Services and are graciously pleased to make ordain and establish the

• • • • • • • • • • • • • • • • •

as if the acts were done under his own eye.—

Fourteenthly. It is ordained that every Warrant Officer Petty Officer Seaman or Marine or Non-Commissioned Officer or Soldier who shall have received the Cross shall from the date of the act by which

VC Warrent original 1.

the Decoration has been gained be entitled to a Special Pension of Ten Pounds a year; and each additional bar conferred under rule four on such Warrant or Petty Officer or Non-commissioned Officers or Men, shall carry with it an additional pension of Five Pounds per annum.

Fifteenthly. In order to make such additional provision as shall effectually preserve pure this Most Honorable distinction it is ordained that if any person on whom such distinction shall be conferred be convicted of Treason Cowardice, Felony or of any infamous Crime, or if he be accused of any such offence and doth not after a reasonable time surrender himself to be tried for the same his name shall forthwith be erased from the Registry of Individuals upon whom the said Decoration shall have been conferred by an especial Warrant under Our Royal Sign Manual, and the pension conferred under rule fourteen shall cease and determine from the date of such Warrant. It is hereby further declared that We Our Heirs and Successors shall be the sole judges of the circumstance demanding such expulsion; moreover We shall at all times have power to restore such persons as may at any time have been expelled, both to the enjoyment of the Decoration and Pension.

Given at Our Court at Buckingham Palace this twenty ninth day of January in the Nineteenth Year of Our Reign and in the Year of Our Lord One Thousand Eight Hundred and Fifty Six

By Her Majesty's Command

Panmure

To Our Principal Secretary of State for War

VC Warrent, original 2.

The London Gazette

The London Gazette is the official newspaper of record for Great Britain, published by H.M. Stationary Office, in which certain statutory notices are published. It was not a conventional newspaper offering general news coverage but as it was first published on 7 November 1665 it can claim to be Britain's oldest continuously published newspaper.

Numb. 21971.   649

SUPPLEMENT
TO
The London Gazette
Of TUESDAY the 24th of FEBRUARY.

Published by Authority.

TUESDAY, FEBRUARY 24, 1857.

War Office, 24th February, 1857.

THE Queen has been graciously pleased to signify Her intention to confer the Decoration of the Victoria Cross on the undermentioned Officers and Men of Her Majesty's Navy and Marines, and Officers, Non-commissioned Officers, and Men of Her Majesty's Army, who have been recommended to Her Majesty for that Decoration, —in accordance with the rules laid down in Her Majesty's Warrant of the 29th of January, 1856— on account of acts of bravery performed by them before the Enemy during the late War, as recorded against their several names, viz.:—

ROYAL NAVY (INCLUDING THE NAVAL BRIGADE EMPLOYED ON SHORE) AND ROYAL MARINES.

Name and Rank.	Act of Bravery for which recommended.
Cecil William Buckley, Commander	Lord Lyons reports that—" Whilst serving as junior Lieutenant of the 'Miranda,' this Officer landed in presence of a superior force, and set fire to the Russian stores at Genitchi;" and " he also performed a similar *desperate service* at Taganrog." The first service referred to occurred after the shelling of the town of Genitchi, on the 29th May, 1855. After mentioning that the stores were in a very favourable position for supplying the Russian Army, and that, therefore, their destruction was of the utmost importance, Captain Lyons writes: "Lieutenant Cecil W. Buckley, Lieutenant Hugh T. Burgoyne, and Mr. John Roberts, gunner, volunteered to land alone, and fire the stores, which offer I accepted, knowing the imminent risk there would be in landing a party in presence of such a superior force, and out of gun-shot of the ships. This very dangerous service they most gallantly performed, narrowly escaping the Cossacks, who all but cut them off from their boat." (Despatch from Admiral Lord Lyons, 2nd June, 1855, No. 419.) The second volunteer service was performed while the town of Taganrog was being bombarded by the boats of the Fleet, and is thus recorded by Captain Lyons :—" Lieutenant Cecil Buckley, in a four-oared gig, accompanied by Mr. Henry Cooper, Boatswain, and manned by volunteers, repeatedly landed and fired the different stores and Government buildings. This dangerous, not to say desperate service (carried out in a town containing upwards of 3,000 troops, constantly endeavouring to prevent it, and only checked by the fire of the boats' guns), was most effectually performed." (Despatch from Admiral Lord Lyons, 6th June, 1855, No. 420.)

London Gazette, First VC.

Issue number 21,971 dated Tuesday, 24 February 1857, was given over entirely to the first eighty-five recipients of the Victoria Cross. Heading the list were most of the officers and men of the Royal Navy who were awarded the VC while serving on shore as part of the Naval Brigade both in the Crimea and the Baltic Sea. Since the Royal Navy had been confined to ineffectively bombarding the forts guarding the entrance to Sebastopol harbour, they brought their heavy guns ashore and were far more effective augmenting the Army's lighter artillery.

Due to the delay of five months on the Queen's part, only fifty-three recipients were still on Home Duty. Subsequent VC *Gazette* entries that were published included four on 5 May 1857 and five on 23 June 1857, making a total of sixty-two who were able to attend the first investiture.

There were fifteen naval personnel including the Royal Marines, and forty-eight from the Army. The latter's first to be awarded was Sergeant-Major John Grieve of the Royal Scots Grays, who took part in the lesser-known Charge of the Heavy Brigade. The Cavalry were followed by the Artillery, the Engineers and finally the Infantry proceeded by the Guards regiments. Apart from a handful of recipients who had left the service, there were two who still wore a uniform of a different kind. George Waters wore the tall hat and plain blue of a police constable and Robert Shields wore the green livery of a 'gate' or park keeper.

Those who were serving abroad were presented with their Crosses by their commanders in chief at special parades. Each general officer was instructed to report the proceedings and send them to the War Office. During the 1880s, the reports were forwarded to the Garter King at Arms.

The London Gazette has continued to publish the Victoria Cross awards from 1857, with the most recent in 2015.

Cecil Buckley – The First Gazetted VC

Born in Manchester in 1828, Cecil William Buckley joined the Royal Navy in his mid-teens. Sent to the American Station, he was involved in intercepting slave ships from West Africa and attacking a Brazilian slave fort at the mouth of the River Paranagua.

He was the first name to appear in *The London Gazette* by virtue that he served in the Senior Service and that his name was alphabetically first. He was serving aboard the steam corvette HMS *Miranda*, which was shelling Russian stores at Genitchi in the Sea of Azov. He landed with two other volunteers, Lieutenant Hugh Burgoyne from *Swallow* and Gunner John Robarts from *Ardent*, destroying a corn store and ammunition dumps while under fire. He also made a similar raid with Boatswain Henry Cooper at the town of Taganrog, destroying the enemy's supplies before narrowly escaping. All these men were awarded the VC.

Buckley was given command of the steam sloop *Merlin* and served on the Cape of Good Hope Station, thus missing the opportunity of being invested by the Queen. Instead he received his VC from Admiral Sir Henry Keppel, who put him in command of his flagship, *Forte*, in 1860. He went to command HMS *Pylades* on

Buckley, C, VC Reverse.

Buckley, C.W.

CECIL WILLIAM
BUCKLEY V.C. R.N.
BORN 7 OCT 1828 - SOMERSET
DIED 7 DEC 1872 - FUNCHAL

THE FIRST VICTORIA CROSS
TO BE ANNOUNCED IN
THE LONDON GAZETTE
24 FEB 1857
FOR GALLANTRY - SEA OF AZOV
CRIMEAN WAR 1855

Buckley, Cecil, Memorial 001.

the Pacific Station and during a survey of the coast of British Columbia he gave his name to one of the features, Buckley Point.

In 1872, he became ill and was forced to retire from the service. Accompanied by his wife and family, Buckley went to Funchal in Madeira, where he died on 7 December 1872. The following day he was laid to rest in the British Cemetery.

On 25 February 2007 a memorial was installed at the English Church of Holy Trinity, Funchal, attended by some 600 people. Johnson Beharry VC travelled to the island to unveil this significant memorial. Cecil Buckley's VC medal group was purchased by King George V and is the only example in the Royal Collection.

The First VC

On 21 June 1854, the lightly armed warships, HMS *Hecla, Valorous* and *Odin* attacked the formidable walls of the Russian fortress at Bomarsund in the Baltic Sea. It was an unequal contest, with the British ships expending their ammunition to little effect. This minor bombardment was significant due to an act of outstanding gallantry by a 20-year old midshipman, or mate, named Charles Davis Lucas.

A live shell, its burning fuse hissing, landed on the deck of *Hecla*. A cry went up for all hands to fling themselves on the deck. One man ignored this sound advice and ran forward, picked up the round shell with its fizzing fuse, carried it to the rail and dropped it overboard. It exploded before it hit the water, wounding two crewmen. Charles Lucas' bravery was quickly recognised when his captain, William Hall, promoted him to acting lieutenant.

His prompt action in saving the lives of his fellow crew was recognised by the Royal Humane Society when they voted to present Lucas with the large 51mm diameter silver medallion, which was not intended for wearing. In 1869, a 38mm diameter medal was produced and presented to Lucas, although this shows it was upgraded to gold.

When it came to the awarding of new Victoria Cross, Lucas' name was submitted. He stood fourth in line at the Hyde Park Investiture to receive a second award for the same action. Lieutenant Charles Lucas saw no further action in his naval career and steadily climbed the promotion ladder before retiring as a rear admiral.

Lucas, Charles medal group.

Lucas, Charles VC.

His retirement brought little peace of mind. To his horror, he left his VC medal group on a train. They have never been recovered and he was issued with a set of unnamed replacement medals.

As if this was not enough, he was summoned to the deathbed of his former captain, now Admiral Sir William Hall, who made the extraordinary request for Lucas to look after his wife and marry his daughter, Frances. Settling in Tunbridge Wells, the marriage was not a success because Frances was arrogant and violent tempered, and far too aware of her being the granddaughter of the 6th Viscount Torrington.

Charles Lucas died a week before the outbreak of the First World War and was interred in his wife's family plot at Mereworth near Maidstone.

Lucas, Charles VC Action.

The First Investiture

The first presentation of the VC took place in Hyde Park on the hot and sunny morning of Friday, 26 June 1857, when Queen Victoria personally decorated sixty-two men who had been selected for outstanding valour against the Russians. Lord Panmur had written to the Queen on 17 February asking how she wanted the VC conferred and received an unsatisfactory reply in which she said that: '…she would confer the new award in person but not until later in the season.'

There was then a lapse until early June, when Panmur wrote to remind Her Majesty of this important event. Four days later, on 12 June, she sent a reply from Windsor in which she had '…come to the conclusion that it would be best to have a Review in Hyde Park where she could attend on horseback and give the Crosses to the recipients … The day might be the 26th inst.' This gave the normally slow-moving Whitehall just sixteen days to organise what was to be the largest Royal occasion to date.

Stands and pavilions had to be ordered and constructed, the 9,000 review troops had to be organised and transported, Hancocks had to prepare and engrave the names of the nine additional VCs published in the recent *London Gazette* (5 May and 23 June) and, most, importantly, the recipients had to be contacted and brought to London. Around 7,000 dignitaries filled the special galleries set in a large semi-circle around the ceremony, leaving the 100,000 public at a distance of half a mile

Queen Victoria's Uniform.

Victoria, The First Investiture.

on the far side of the parade ground with little to see. The Queen and her entourage dressed in military uniforms, departed at 9.30 am and rode the short distance from Buckingham Palace, through Grosvenor Gate at Hyde Park Corner and into the assembled multitude at the southern end of Hyde Park. The day was significant for other reasons. Other than the investiture, her husband was to be henceforth known as Prince Consort. She was also accompanied by the Crown Prince Frederick William of Prussia, soon to marry Vicky, her eldest daughter. It had been expected that the Queen would dismount and present the Crosses from a dais. Instead she chose to remain mounted on her pony 'Sunset'. The investiture took no more than ten minutes to complete, which was an average of ten seconds to decorate each recipient. The newly decorated recipients then moved to form a line about 50 yards in front of the Queen. The review troops then marched between the Queen and the recipients, accompanied by the regimental bands. Finally, the artillery gave a salute, the Royal party departed and arrived back at the Palace around 11.45 am. This significant Royal event had taken a mere two hours to complete.

The Reaction to the New Award

Queen Victoria wrote in her diary of the events of 26 June, concluding with: 'It was indeed a most proud and Gratifying day.' For the spectators it had been very colourful, and even if they were unable to see anything of the investiture, the bright uniforms and bands made it a day to remember. Unfortunately, the new Victoria Cross did not measure up to the expectations of the public and this was voiced in the 27 June edition of *The Times*, whose reporter wrote enthusiastically about the spectacle but gave a negative opinion of the medal: 'Would we ever forget it! Never did we see such a dull, heavy, and tasteless affair. Nor do we suspect that if it was on sale in any town in England at a penny a piece, hardly a dozen would have been sold in a twelvemonth. There is a cross, and a lion, and a scroll or two worked up into the most shapeless mass that the size admits of Valour must, and doubtless will, be still its own reward in this country, for the Victoria Cross is the shabbiest of all prizes.'

Time changed the attitude towards the Victoria Cross and its worth in terms of outstanding bravery gave it cachet that set it apart from all other gallantry awards.

Another lesser but vital matter was how the Queen would pin the Crosses on to the recipients. It is not clear who suggested the method but Prince Albert wrote to Lord Panmure on 19 June 1857: 'The pins attached to the VC, as in the specimen submitted, will answer very well. The Queen has tried them and found them to do so.' This simple method was also the most painful for some recipients. In order for the

Graham, Gerald, Crimea.

Monarch or General Officer Commanding to quickly and smoothly pin the medal to the breast of the recipient, a simple double-prong pin was employed. Afterwards, the recipients would then have a safety broach fitted so it would stay securely fastened to the tunic.

There are several incidents in which the recipients were impaled by this crude but quick method of presenting the VC. Commander Henry Raby, as the first in line at the Hyde Park Investiture, is said to have experienced regal heavy handiness as Queen Victoria leant forward to plant her new award on his tunic. She had chosen to remain mounted, which was

Raby, Henry Crimea.

VC early fixing.

not a stable platform to perform such a task, and her pony shifted slightly, digging the double prong fixing into Raby's chest. A similar thing is supposed to have happened to Private Henry Hook, one of the Rorke's Drift VCs, when he received his Cross uniquely at Rorke's Drift from General Sir Garnet Wolseley.

Lieutenant Gerald Graham (later General Sir Gerald Graham) was twenty-fourth in line at the first investiture. He wrote to his family: 'We were formed in line and then advanced singly to the Queen, who remained on horseback. She pinned the medal with her own hand to our coats. She stuck the pin fairly into me, so I keenly realised my momentary interview with Royalty!'

The Netley Hospital VC

It can be argued that the first presentation of the Victoria Cross did not take place at Hyde Park on 26 June 1857 but at a building site by Southampton Water on 19 May 1856. One of the recommendations made by one of the many commissions sent to the Crimea to investigate the inadequacies of the Army Medical Department was that a purpose-built military hospital should be built for the sick and wounded of Queen Victoria's army. The site chosen was on the Netley Grange Estate, which the owner sold to the government.

Construction began in 1856 and Queen Victoria was invited to lay the foundation stone, her first public engagement after the end of the Crimean War. She arrived from Osborne House on the Royal Yacht on 19 May 1856 with members of her family to open the new hospital, named the Royal Victoria Hospital but later commonly referred to as the Netley Hospital.

VC Netley, Victoria laying foundation stone.

VC Reverse from Netley.

She inspected the plans, which were then placed in a copper casket along with a document signed by the Queen, coins of the realm, a four-bar Crimea War medal and an unnamed Victoria Cross. The casket was then placed within the foundation stone, which was suspended by a golden rope before being lowered into a bed of mortar.

When the hospital was eventually opened on 11 March 1863, it was the world's longest building, being a quarter of a mile long, and contained 1,000 beds. Impressive from the exterior, it hid many flaws that Florence Nightingale highlighted. Despite the drawbacks in its interior design, Netley served the wounded and sick soldiers until the 1950s, when it was closed. A fire demolished part of the empty shell and it was decided to demolish the building in September 1966.

In December that year members of the Army Medical Services gathered for the raising of the foundation stone and the anticipation of what lay within the casket. Besides the plans and documents, the main attraction was the two unnamed medals placed in the casket by Victoria. After much deliberation, it was decided to have both medals suitably engraved to establish their identity. Hancocks engraved what was in effect the first presentation VC with the following text:

On the bar: *Placed by H.M. Queen Victoria in Foundations R.Vic.Hospital, Netley*

On the centre of the reverse: *Sited 19 May 1856. Recovered 7 Dec 1966*

The Only Officer VC of the Light Brigade

orn 15 September 1833 at York (now Toronto), Alexander Dunn was the fifth son of the Receiver-General of Upper Canada. In March 1852 at 19 years of age, he was purchased a commission into the 11th (Prince Albert's Own Regiment) Hussars. The uniform was of the finest in the Light Cavalry, courtesy of its wealthy commander, Lord Cardigan. When the regiment was sent to the Crimea, Cardigan was made Commander

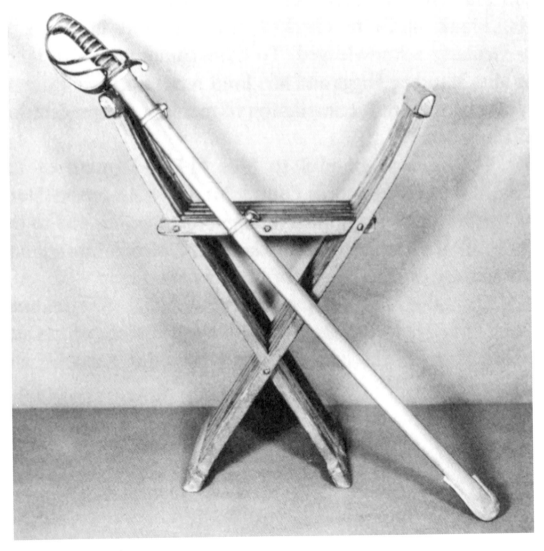

Dunn, extra-long sword.

Dunn, Alexander, Charge of the Light Brigade VC.

of the Light Brigade and the command of the regiment devolved on Lieutenant-Colonel John Douglas.

Alexander Dunn was tall for a light cavalryman, 6ft 2in, and described as handsome, good-natured and a dandy. To accommodate his height and reach, he had Wilkinson Sword make him a 4ft-long sabre several inches longer than the regulation weapon. This formidable side arm was used to good effect as the 11th began to withdraw up the North Valley. Douglas had managed to keep his men together and they attempted to ride clear of the encircling Russian cavalry. As they were attempting this, Dunn spotted Sergeant Robert Bentley wrestling with his horse, which had been severely wounded

and was falling behind. Seeing his predicament, Dunn wheeled round and spurred through the confusion of bodies, living and dead, to rescue him. With his thoroughbred mount rearing and side-wheeling in panic, Dunn slashed and thrust at three assailants until he had killed them. With Bentley's mount unable to carry him, Dunn dismounted and placed him into his own saddle, then slapped the horse on the rump to send it galloping after the rest his regiment.

Now on foot, Dunn rushed to the assistance of Private Harvey Levitt from his troop, who had lost his horse and was being attacked by an enemy hussar. A quick powerful thrust dispatched the Russian and both men made their escape.

Dunn applied to sell his commission just two weeks after the Battle of Balaclava. Despite Cardigan's attempt to block his resignation, Dunn did leave the Army. He then returned to his family's large estates in Canada. There may have been another reason for departing England and the Regiment so precipitously, for he absconded with Colonel Douglas' wife, Rosa, some years senior to him. A hurt and humiliated Douglas refused to grant her a divorce.

When the regiments selected their Victoria Crosses, the 11th Hussars chose Alexander Dunn. It must have been a most awkward situation for the sorely tried Colonel Douglas. The errant hero returned to England to receive his Cross from the Queen at Hyde Park on 26 June 1857. He later raised the 100th (Prince of Wales Royal Canadian) Regiment and was the youngest colonel in the British Army. He transferred to the 33rd Regiment and was killed in a hunting accident while on campaign in Abyssinia in 1868, and was buried at Senafe.

The Blockade Runner VCs

Two twenty-year old Royal Navy officers were awarded the Victoria Cross during the Crimea War. Lieutenant William Nathan Hewett was in command of a two-gun battery on the British right above Inkerman when a 4,000-strong Russian force left Sebastopol and climbed the steep Careening Pass. They pushed aside the British pickets towards the lightly defended part of the British line. A call to spike his guns and retreat had Hewett ignoring the order and manoeuvring his 68-pounder Lancaster so the muzzle was against the parapet. He blew away the earthworks, giving him a clear arc of fire. With his gun fully depressed, he poured deadly grapeshot followed by solid shot, which had the Russian in full retreat.

Lieutenant Hugh Talbot Burgoyne was one of a three-man party, led by Cecil Buckley, in a successful raid that destroyed Russian supplies in the ports on the Sea of Azov.

Post-Crimea, both officers commanded ships on the North American and West Indies Station. This coincided with the Civil War between the American northern and southern states, which interrupted Britain's import of cotton from the Confederacy. Although the British Government appeared neutral, they clandestinely supported the South. A number of fast paddle steamers were built in British shipyards and a few highly skilled Royal Navy seamen were put on half-pay and given command of these 'blockade runners' to run the gauntlet of the Federal Navy patrolling the Confederate coast.

Blockade runner civil war.

Hewett (seated 2 right) and Burgoyne (3 right) and Blockade Runners.

Captains Hewett and Burgoyne assumed the pseudonyms of 'Samuel S. Ridge' and 'Captain Talbot' respectively. It should be pointed out that their actions were not entirely altruistic as they were rewarded with $5,000 in gold.

Hugh Burgoyne made two or three successful 'runs' in 1864. William Hewett was given command of the fast, low-profile side-wheel steamer *Condor*, which met with disaster on her last run. On 10 August 1864, she sailed from Greenock carrying the Confederate Commissioner in London and Mrs Rose O'Neal Greenhow, 'Wild Rose', the Confederacy's renowned spy and propagandist.

They were pursued by a Union gunboat and *Condor* ran aground at the mouth of Cape Fear River, North Carolina. As they rowed ashore, the dinghy was swamped and 'Wild Rose', weighed down by the gold she was carrying, drowned. Hewett and his crew were taken captive but were released having promised never to run the blockade again.

Both VCs died young; Burgoyne, aged 37, when his new ship, *Captain*, foundered off Cape Finistère in 1870 and Hewett at the age of 54 at the Haslar Hospital in 1888.

The One-Armed VC

One of the outstanding soldiers of the Crimea War was John Simpson Knox. Born in Glasgow in 1828, he was the son of a sergeant in the British Army. His childhood was unhappy and, at the age of 14, he ran away to enlist in the Scots Fusilier Guards. Because of his height he was able to persuade the recruiting officers that he was older and by the time he was 18, he had been promoted to corporal.

At the Battle of the Alma, he was appointed colour sergeant and averted panic that appeared among the Guards and Light Division as they climbed the slope towards the main Russian bastion. With order restored, the Russians were driven out of their main battery and the battle was all but over. Knox was again involved at Balaclava and fought in the deadly fight for the Sandbag Battery at Inkerman.

Knox's exceptional leadership skills had not gone unnoticed and he was recommended for a commission without purchase into the Rifle Brigade. On 18 June 1856, he led a ladder party in the assault on the Great Redan, the formidable strong point before Sebastopol. Reaching the abattis below the Russian position, Lieutenant Knox attempted to shoot at the enemy, only to receive a musket ball that smashed his left arm. Forced to retreat, he was again hit in the left arm by some grapeshot including a 53mm diameter projectile that embedded in his arm. The surgeons could not save his arm, which was amputated; according to Knox, without chloroform. Against the odds, Knox survived. He kept the grapeshot as a memento and had it mounted on a marble plinth engraved 'Crimea, Sebastopol, Redan, June 18, 1855.'

He received his VC at the first investiture and was singled out for mention in Victoria's diary of that day. After retiring as major in 1872, he became Governor of Cardiff and Liverpool prisons until 1892. He retired to Cheltenham, where he died in 1897.

Knox, J, cannon ball.

Knox, John Simpson VC Rifles.

Howard Elphinstone – Queen Victoria's Trusted Confidant

Howard Craufurd Elphinstone was born in his family's estate near Riga, Livornia (now Latvia). His stay in this Baltic state was short-lived as the lease on the estate expired in 1830 and the Elphinstones embarked on a nomadic life, moving around the Continent until 1844, when they returned to England. This unconventional life gave young Howard a mastery of languages and a broader view on life than many of his contemporaries. Through connections, Howard managed to enter the Royal Military Academy, finishing top of his class to emerge as an officer in the Royal Engineers. He went to the Crimea and was involved in constructing gun batteries and the trench system that crept towards the Russian lines at Sebastopol.

On 17 June 1855 one of the Army's worst wastage of human life occurred as hundreds of men stumbled up the half-mile slope towards the guns of the Great Redan. Soon the hillside was littered with dead and wounded men. Elphinstone had not charged but that evening he gathered together six men at gunpoint to follow him to collect any surviving wounded. In the fading light, they found twenty wounded and much of the discarded equipment. Three months later, on 8 September, another attempt was made to storm the Redan. In the exchange of fire, a Russian shell landed close to Lieutenant Elphinstone, throwing debris into his face and costing him the sight of his left eye.

Returning to England, Elphinstone was recommended to act as a military governor for the Royal Family's 11-year-old son, Prince Alfred. Although not among the first crop of recipients and despite his elevation to the royal household, Elphinstone was deservedly awarded the Victoria Cross, something that sparked controversy at the time. On 2 August 1858, he was among twelve recipients who lined up on Southsea Common near Portsmouth.

Elphinstone, Howard, silver mounted miniature belonging to HRH.

SS 'Tongariro'.

As he settled into his role he was given an additional governorship to oversee the development of Prince Leopold, the Queen's fourth son. His years with the Royal Family saw Victoria's battle with the Prussian court, the death of Prince Albert, the Queen's prolonged period of mourning, Leopold's haemophilia and the unsettling effect John Brown had on the royal courtiers. He accompanied his charges on their trips to Canada, the USA, the Middle East and Russia. Over the years, Victoria came to regard Elphinstone as her confidant and friend. He was knighted and in 1876, the aging bachelor married a 19-year-old beauty. During his time with the Royal Family, he was showered with presents, culminating in a Stradivarius violin. As for the Queen, she commissioned and wore a silver-mounted portrait of Elphinstone, which was found amongst her belongings when she died.

Howard suffered from bronchitis and in 1890 the family decided to travel to the warmer climate of Tenerife. They sailed on the steamer SS *Tongariro*, which hit rough seas as she entered the Bay of Biscay. Howard and a companion were standing near the wheelhouse when the

Elphinstone, Howard.

ship made a heavy roll and Elphinstone was catapulted 15ft to the lower deck, where he lay by an open port. Another roll and he was pitched into the sea; his body was never found. The captain gave the family his chart with the exact spot of the tragedy: Ushant light bearing S. by E. distant 22 miles.

Sir Henry Clifford VC and Crimea War Artist

In what is now recognised as one of the best personal records of a serving officer in the Crimea, Henry Clifford kept a journal and, over the following two years, made 120 watercolour paintings, which graphically illustrate the horror and bleakness of the Crimean campaign. As a staff officer, Henry was an accurate witness to the Battles of the Alma and Sebastopol. At Balaclava he watched horror struck as the Light Brigade rode to its destruction and immortality. It was as the onset of the Crimean winter began to bite that Henry Clifford performed the exploit that led to him being one of the first recipients of the Victoria Cross.

On 5 November, on the heights above Sebastopol, the bloody and confused fight known

Clifford, Henry, Crimean VC.

Clifford, Henry, Sketsh of burial party.

as Inkerman was contested. Henry Clifford later wrote of his part in the battle: 'On reaching the left brow of the hill, I saw the enemy in great numbers in our front, about 15 yards from us; it was a moment or two before I could make General Buller believe that they were Russians. "In God's name," I said, "fix bayonets and charge." He gave the order and in another moment we were hand to hand with them. Our line was not long enough to prevent the Russians outflanking us on our left, which was unperceived by the 77th, who rushed on, with the exception of about a dozen, who, struck by the force on our left and who saw me taking out my revolver, halted with me.

'"Come on," I said, "my lads!" and the brave fellows dashed in amongst the astonished Russians, bayoneting them in every direction. One of the bullets in my revolver had partly come out and prevented it revolving and I could not get it off. The Russians fired their pieces off within a few yards of my head, but none touched me. I drew my sword and cut off one man's arm who was in the act of bayoneting me and a second seeing it, turned around and was in the act of running out of my way, when I hit him over the back of the neck and laid him dead at my feet. About 15 of them threw down their arms and gave themselves up and the remainder ran back and fell into the hands of the 77th returning from the splendid charge they had made and were killed or taken prisoners.'

Next day, Clifford wrote: 'This morning, as I passed the Russians, prisoners and wounded, a man amongst them ran up and called out to me and pointed to his shoulder bound up. It was the poor fellow whose arm I had cut off yesterday; he laughed and said, "Bono Johnny."'

Clifford went on to serve in China and Africa and was appointed Governor of Natal at the end of the Zulu War. He returned home and retired as a major-general, dying on 12 April 1883 at his home in Devon.

William Peel – The Premature End of A Naval Hero

One of the most remarkable seamen of his age was William Peel, the third son of Sir Robert Peel, the Prime Minister. Without the patronage of his father, he succeeded in attaining the rank of captain by the age of 25, the youngest captain in the Royal Navy. He was in command of the twenty-eight-gun sloop HMS *Diamond* when his crew constructed and manned two gun batteries to bombard Sebastopol. While volunteers carried kegs of powder into the gun placements, a Russian 42-pounder shell with its burning fuse landed amongst the powder cases. A shout of alarm alerted Peel and he lifted the heavy shell and staggered to the parapet. As he hefted it over barricade, the shell exploded but caused no loss of life. Shortly afterwards, he was on hand to warn the Guards fighting in the Sandbag Battery at Inkerman that the Russians were about to surround them. His third act of valour was during the abortive attack on the Redan on 18 June 1855 when he led his Naval Brigade ladder party to the foot of the Russian batteries. Badly wounded in the arm, he was led away by his two young aides; Edward Daniel, who received the VC, and Evelyn Wood, who did not. Peel was invalided home and recommended for the Victoria Cross. His citation appeared in the first VC supplement of *The London Gazette* of 24 February 1857.

While convalescing at his home in Sandy, Bedfordshire, he was asked by the people of Potten if he would build a railway to connect their town with the main London line at Sandy. This he was able to do and the branch line was

Peel, William, posing with his naval dirk.

completed in June 1857, being officially opened by his mother. Peel also purchased a locomotive at the cost of £800 which he named *Shannon* after his newly built frigate HMS *Shannon*. He missed the opening as he was on his way to China but was diverted to India to help suppress the Sepoy Mutiny. Under his leadership, his Naval Brigade served with great distinction, with five members of his crew receiving the Victoria Cross; Nowell Salmon, John Harrison, Edward Robinson, William Hall and Thomas Young.

During the campaign, Peel received the KCB and was appointed ADC to the Queen. His Victoria Cross began its protracted journey; first

Peel, William, dirk.

Peel, William, locomotive Shannon. Sandy Railway Centre.

to Hong Kong, then India and back to London. In the interim, William Peel had been wounded and contracted smallpox from which he died. There were few troops in Cawnpore at the time to form a burial party and only two people attended his funeral; a sad and inappropriate way to celebrate the life of one of Britain's greatest naval heroes.

Louis Desanges – VC Artist

Louis William Desanges was an artist born in London in 1822, the great grandson of a French nobleman who sought refuge in England. Desanges made his living painting portraits of women and children but, soon after the VC Investiture at Hyde Park, he began to produce paintings to illustrate the actions of the first recipients. His first two were of Private Samuel Parkes (4th Light Dragoon) and Corporal Robert Shields (23rd Regiment) representing the cavalry and infantry respectively. Although his paintings were wooden and unconvincing, he was skilled with capturing the sitter's likeness, making them historically important.

He went on to paint a total of forty-six canvases of Crimean and Indian Mutiny VCs, favouring junior officers. Later he did paint a few others, including a large canvas of Major-General Sir Frederick Robert's march from

Desanges, Raby VC with John Taylor VC and Henry Curtis VC carrying wounded soldier.

Desanges, Lindsay, Robert Crimean VC.

Desanges, Lindsay, Robert Major.

Kabul to Kandahar in 1880. It is quite likely that Royal patronage had been forthcoming, for the collection was put on exhibition variously at the Egyptian Hall in Piccadilly, the Crystal Palace and Alexandra Palace.

By the end of the century the collection was put up for sale. One of the Crimean VCs, Robert Lindsay of the Scots Fusilier Guards, was one of the wealthiest landowners in England and ennobled as Lord Wantage. He was unhappy that the paintings were being dispersed and purchased the remaining paintings for £1,000. Some of the paintings had already been bought by family members, some by the regiments and in the case of Canadian-born Lieutenant Alexander Dunn, by the Government of Ontario.

Lord Wantage offered his collection of forty-six paintings to the town of Wantage and the council accepted, making the Corn Exchange available for the paintings and renaming it the

Victoria Cross Gallery. Lord Wantage paid for the restoration and hanging but came into conflict with the council when he wanted the paintings illuminated by electric light, whereas the council insisted on gas lighting. It turned out that Lord Wantage was a major shareholder in the London Electric Supply Corporation, while the council owned the Wantage Gas Works!

The exhibition remained open for the next forty years. When the Second World War started, the Ministry of Food requisitioned the hall as a cooking depot and the paintings were stored away and forgotten. When they were rediscovered in 1951, there had been several casualties through water damage. Among those campaigning to keep the collection together was John Betjeman but the cost was too much and the paintings were offered on permanent loan to museums and military authorities. Wantage Council did keep one painting; Captain Robert Lindsay VC. Desange's paintings are frequently used to illustrate books about the VC and his output has proved to be invaluable to historians.

Thomas Kavanagh's Disguise

Thomas Henry Kavanagh became one of the most celebrated VCs of the Victorian period. He was born in County Westmeath, Ireland in 1821, the son of the bandmaster of the 3rd Regiment. In 1834, the family moved to India and, in 1839, Thomas started work as a clerk in various government departments. Despite gradually moving up the Civil Service promotion ladder, he experienced financial hardship, due mainly to his large family of ten children.

When the Indian Mutiny broke out in May 1857, Kavanagh and his family took refuge with 1,280 non-combatants in the grounds and buildings of the British Residency in Lucknow. The male civilians were called upon to help the 1,500 loyal native troops and the soldiers of the 32nd Regiment to defend the extensive barricades around the Residency. Kavanagh was very active in this role and, as the siege dragged on, he saw this crisis as a means to pull himself out of his poverty trap.

In September, General Havelock's troops did force their way into the Residency compound but were too few in number to achieve a relief and became besieged themselves. In November, an Indian messenger named Kunoujee Lal brought a despatch from Sir Colin Campbell's large relief column. The Residency's senior officers drew up a route that Sir Colin should take to avoid the narrow streets of the city. It needed someone with knowledge of the area to explain it to the relief force. To Kavanagh this was the opportunity he sought.

Kavanagh, Kanouji Lal, his guide.

Donning an Indian disguise and using lamp-black to cover his freckled white skin, Kavanagh passed the test of his peers. Along with Kunoujee Lal, who had been promised a substantial reward if he accompanied the Irishman, they slipped away during the evening. A series of adventures and narrow escapes finally brought the couple to the camp of the relieving force. The message was delivered and Sir Colin Campbell was able to fight his way

Kavanagh, T VC disguise.

Kavanagh, Thomas, India.

into the Residency with fewer casualties thanks to Kavanagh's guidance.

At the end of the Mutiny, Kavanagh was rewarded with what he considered a miserly sum of £2,000 and this rankled with him until his dying day. He was also nominated for a Victoria Cross but this was refused as the Royal Warrant stated it could only be conferred on military personnel. After much lobbying, it was amended and Kavanagh along with two other civilians, Ross Mangles and William McDonnel, received the Cross. Despite the public adulation, Kavanagh felt that the VC had been given grudgingly. He wrote a book entitled *How I Won the Victoria Cross*, which sold well but there were detractors who accused him of self-aggrandisement and profiting from his deed. Nevertheless, Kavanagh was regarded as one of the greatest heroes of the Victorian age. He died on 11 November 1882 at Gibraltar while visiting a fellow Lucknow defender, Sir Robert Napier.

Thomas Butler's Colt Revolver

Born in Hampshire in 12 February 1836, Thomas Adair Butler was privately educated before being commissioned in the Honourable East India Company's Army in 1854. He joined the 1st Bengal (European) Fusiliers and was involved in most of the significant battles of the Indian Mutiny. Lieutenant Butler was awarded his Victoria Cross in early 1858 during the final assault and capture of Lucknow. After a heavy British bombardment across the Goomtee River, it seemed the enemy lines were deserted but it was necessary to get this information to the 79th Highlanders, who were about 600 yards away on the far bank. In order to discover whether the enemy were in occupation, Butler volunteered to

Butler, Thomas.

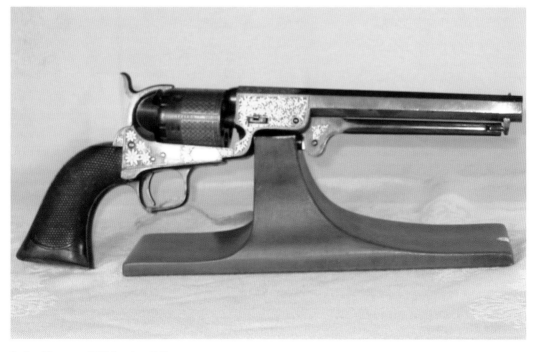

Butler, Thomas. 1851 London Colt.

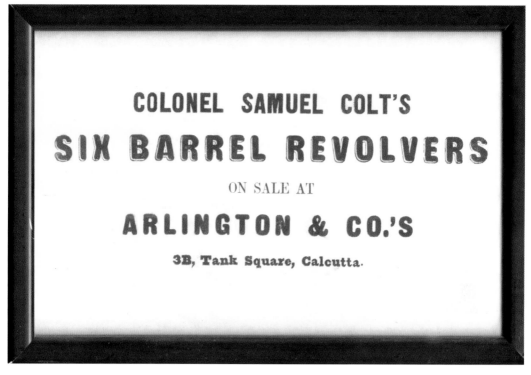

COLONEL SAMUEL COLT'S

SIX BARREL REVOLVERS

ON SALE AT

ARLINGTON & CO.'S

3B, Tank Square, Calcutta.

Butler, Thos. Colt handbill.

swim the filthy Goomtee – worth an award in itself – to gather this vital information. This he managed to do under fire and inform the 79th Highlanders.

Previous to the outbreak of the Mutiny, Butler had purchased a London-made Colt 1851 Model Revolver, probably from Colt's representative Arlington and Co. in Calcutta. Young Butler took advantage of the cheap local artisans to have his gun decorated with foliate and floral gold panels. The rear sides of the frame were adorned with gold flower blossoms with platinum branches. It is not believed that Colt ever produced such decoration on its revolvers, but it is known that individual officers had them decorated in India. Later he had the backstrap engraved with 'Thomas Adair Butler/101st Regiment'.

The weapon was not only pretty in appearance but Butler used it to shoot an enemy at close range. His regiment was disbanded in 1861 and re-emerged as Her Majesty's 101st Regiment (Royal Bengal Fusiliers) and he no doubt carried it when he went on the Umbeyla Expedition in 1863. He retired as major in 1874 and returned to England, where he died in 1901 at Camberley.

The Bizarre Death of George William Drummond Stewart VC

The family affairs of the 6th Baronet of Murthly and Blair were highly complicated. William Drummond Stewart was the second son who chose the Army as a career, while his elder brother became the successor to Murthly Castle, Grantully, Perthshire. William served as an officer with the 15th Hussars at Waterloo but later left. While in Edinburgh, William met a beautiful servant girl named Christine Maria Stewart (no relation) and she had a son born in 1831 named George William Drummond Stewart. Although illegitimate, George was acknowledged by William, who later married Christine, so making his son his heir. For the next dozen years, William travelled the far west of the United States with famous mountain-men such as Tom Fitzpatrick and Jim Bridger. News of his brother's death brought William back to Murthly Castle.

His son barely knew his father but at the age of 17, William purchased a commission for him in the 93rd Sutherland Highland Regiment. Two years later, while he was stationed in Portsmouth, George had

an affair with the daughter of a Southampton merchant and she produced twin boys. The following year the regiment was sent to the Crimea and George's mother and his uncle took responsibility of the twins with the

Stewart, George Drummond VC action.

Stewart, George, presentation Sword.

proviso that George should never make contact with them.

The 93rd gained fame on the slopes of the Alma and at Balaclava by standing firm as the Thin Red Line. With the end of the war against Russia, the regiment was soon sent to India to help suppress the Mutiny. On 16 November 1857, the 93rd was part of Sir Colin Campbell's command as they sought to raise the siege of the Lucknow Residency. One of the strong points that had to be taken was the Secundra Bagh. During the attack on this walled palace, two enemy guns on the flank held up the advance. Captain Stewart called on a few of his men to follow him as he charged straight at the guns before they could reload and they were captured at the point of the bayonet. In the ballot amongst the officers of the 93rd, Stewart was elected to receive the Victoria Cross in a day that saw eighteen awarded; the highest number for a single action.

On his return from India, George Stewart was invited by the tenants of his father's estates to a dinner, where he was presented with a magnificent sword of honour. He decided to leave the Army and there is a mystery about his subsequent activities. He was something of a rake for he made pregnant the daughter of an Edinburgh fishing tackle maker. The complications that would have followed were saved when the infant died.

The twins were now being educated at a boarding school near Southampton and George could not resist observing them from afar. George's bizarre death soon followed. In a fit of drunkenness, he tried to demonstrate the art of sword swallowing with a stick, with fatal consequences. He lingered in agony for two days before dying. His body was taken back to Murthly Castle, where he was buried alongside his mother.

The First Soldier into the Secundrabagh

John Dunley (Dunlay or Dunlea) was born in Douglas, County Cork, in 1831 and is one of those Irish soldiers about whom little is known. He would have lived through the Irish potato famine of the 1840s and sought one of the few opportunities to escape the ravages of that period by taking the 'heroic option' and joining the British Army. Dunley found himself in a Highland regiment, the 93rd Sutherland Highlanders, which had previously drawn its recruits from the local highlanders. The potato famine had spread to Scotland and this combined with the effects of the ongoing Highland clearances had caused recruiting to dry up and led to many Scottish regiments taking many Irish into their ranks.

Dunley's medal entitlement shows that he wore the Indian Mutiny medal with clasps for 'Relief of Lucknow' and 'Lucknow'. He was selected for the VC by ballot and his citation dated 24 December 1858 reads: 'For being the first man, now surviving, of the regiment who on the 16th Nov. 1857, entered one of the breaches in the Secundra Bagh at Lucknow,

Dunley, J. Group of 93rd NCOs 1860.

I GOT THIS BULLET WITH THE VICTORIA CROSS OF JOHN DUNLEY FROM HIS SON. IT WAS TAKEN FROM THE FATHERS KNEE AFTER THE ASSAULT & CAPTURE OF THE FORT OF SECUNDERBAGH Nov. 17. 1857

Nº 12. GREAT BRITAIN VICTORIA CROSS

Dunley, John, medal and bullet.

The Secundra Bagh was defended by hundreds of sepoys, who felt secure behind the substantial castellated walls. The close-range firing of the guns of the Naval Brigade blew a narrow opening through which Lance Corporal Dunley entered to be greeted by heavy firing. In performing this gallant action, he was hit in the knee by a musket ball, which he kept as a memento. He was one of six men of the 93rd who received the VC on 16 November for gallantry at the Secundra Bagh and Shah Najaf. When he returned home, he was presented with his VC by Queen Victoria on 4 January 1860 at Windsor Castle. He left the Army and returned to his native Cork. On 17 October 1890, he died in the South Infirmary of injuries received in an accident. He was buried in an unmarked grave in St Joseph's Cemetery, Cork. Curiously, his Victoria Cross was purchased by the Indian Maharaja of Patiala in the 1920s and is displayed in the Sheesh Mahal, a semi-private museum, along with the VCs of Captain George Fiott Day, Captain of the Forecastle John Taylor, Leading Seaman William Ogers and Private Beach. John Dunley's VC is accompanied by a small engraved plated that states: 'I got this bullet with the Victoria Cross of John Dunley from his son. It was taken from his father's knee after the assault & capture of the fort of Secunderbagh. Nov. 17 (sic). 1857.'

with Capt. Burroughs, whom he most gallantly supported against superior numbers. Elected by the private soldiers of the regiment.'

The Enigma of Rifleman Same Shaw VC

Another private soldier who was awarded the Victoria Cross but has left little of his private life was John (Same) Shaw. Nothing is known of his early life except that he was born on an unknown date at Prestonpans, East Lothian. He enlisted in the Army on 6 April 1849 with his employment listed as a labourer. His service from 1849–54 is not known and he first appears in 1855 on the Rifle Brigade's muster rolls as part of the newly formed 3rd Battalion.

He left with the 3/Rifles for India and joined Sir Colin Campbell's 3,000-strong column in the campaign chasing rebels in Oudh. For eight weeks they moved through hostile country, constantly skirmishing until, on 13 June 1858, they faced a 15,000-strong rebel army at Nawabgunge. Eye-witness accounts reported in the Regimental history graphically describe Shaw's action: 'One man, a Ghazee (Ghazi) being cut off from his companions, seemed determined to make a desperate fight of it. Setting his back against a tree, he stood, sword in hand, glaring fiercely at his pursuers, for some officers and men had followed him

Shaw, John Rifles c.1860.

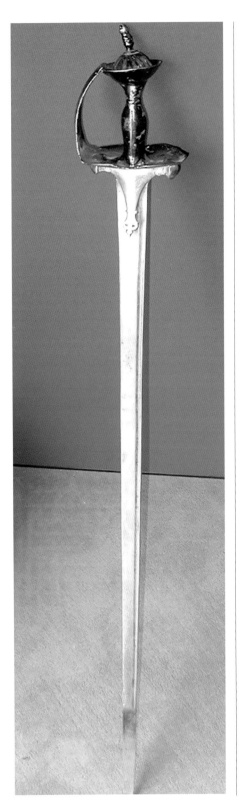

into the *tope* (a stand of trees). Some shots were taken at him, which he tried to avoid by dodging round the tree, but he was wounded and made more desperate. At last a Pioneer of the 3rd Battalion, Samuel (sic) Shaw rushed at him and closed with him. The Ghazee wounded him on the head with his *tulwar* (a sabre) but Shaw, drawing his Pioneer's sword, sawed at him with the serrated back and despatched him. Shaw rose from the ground covered with blood, but his opponent was slain. Many who witnessed it declared that this combat with a fanatic determined to sell his life to slay his foe, was the greatest instance of cool courage they had ever seen.'

John Shaw was immediately recommended for the Victoria Cross and at the end of the Mutiny sailed for England. His VC is engraved with 'Same Shaw', which could stand for Samuel but the rolls show that it was John Shaw who won the VC. Maybe 'Same' was a nickname and put on the VC in error. On 27 December 1859, he committed suicide by jumping overboard, probably in a fit of depression brought on by his head wounds. He never received his Cross, which was probably sent to his next of kin. Amongst his possessions was his adversary's *tulwar*.

Shaw, John (Sam), tulwar.

Sir Samuel Browne – Inventor of a Famous Belt

It took the loss of his left arm for Captain Samuel Browne of 2nd Punjab Irregular Cavalry to realise that he was unable to draw his sword. He was involved in the mopping up operations of the Indian Mutiny in the late summer of 1858, when he was attacked and received two sword cuts; one to the left knee and the other that severed his left arm at the shoulder. He miraculously survived the trauma of the injury and continued to serve in the Indian Army. In the Victorian Army, officers who were badly injured or disabled were not retired as medically unfit unless they were totally incapacitated; officers such as Evelyn Wood VC, who suffered from many complaints including incipient deafness. Similarly, Lieutenant Gonville Bromhead VC, of Rorke's Drift fame, was profoundly deaf and Sir Garnet Wolseley relied on one eye for his entire career. Several one-armed officers, including the previously mentioned John Knox VC, and the much-wounded Adrian Carton de Wiart VC from more recent wars, were able to serve with distinction.

In the Victorian period all officers carried a sword into battle. It hung from the waist-belt by a small metal clip called a 'frog'. The downside was that the scabbard tended to slide around and had to be steadied with the left hand. Having survived the loss of his left arm, Browne found he could not control or draw his sword. He came up with the idea of wearing a second belt that went over his right shoulder and held the scabbard in a leather 'frog' that would hook onto a heavy leather belt. The waist belt also carried

Browne, Sam.

D-rings for attachments and a holstered pistol could be carried on the right side.

Browne's personal innovation was taken up by other cavalry officers in the Indian Army and it soon became part of the standard uniform. Browne never thought to have his invention patented, which would have made him a very rich man. During the Boer War this harness was copied by the Imperial and Commonwealth troops and was standard issue by the First World War.

Samuel James Browne was born in India and entered the Indian Army, taking part in the Second Sikh War of 1848. He was awarded the

Browne, Sam, Belt.

Victoria Cross for gallantry at Seeporah, where he lost his arm. He rose through the ranks to be promoted to general and knighted. He commanded the Peshawar Field Force in the 2nd Afghan War and retired in 1898 having served for nearly sixty years. Despite his military honours, he is best remembered for his brainwave of an invention.

24

Photographs of Two VC Recipients in Death

Photographs of loved ones taken after they died seems very morbid to modern sensibilities. There was a time in the mid-Victorian period that the increased popularity of photography made it acceptable to commemorate the dead and lessen the sharpness of grief. It was a time when so many diseases and epidemics could carry off anybody, leading to memento mori photographic portraiture.

This also applied to men serving in the armed services. One such example is the young Victoria Cross winner, William George Hawtry Bankes. He was the fifth child born to the Right Honourable George Bankes MP and his

Bankes, William.

Lyons, John.

When he was found, he had been severely hacked and was barely alive. Taken to hospital, his right arm and leg were amputated. Sir Colin Campbell had been so impressed by his bravery that he recommended him for the Victoria Cross. Eighteen days later, young Willy Bankes died of blood poisoning due to infected wounds. Propped up and with sightless eyes, an ambrotype was taken and sent to his parents.

Another VC who died young was a rough, tough Irishman named John Lyons of the 19th Regiment. He was with the regiment in the Crimea and took part in the fighting at the Alma when the 19th stormed the Great Redoubt. He was used as a marksman on Victoria Ridge in the Battle of Inkerman and spent the rest of the war in the trenches before Sebastopol. It was here on 11 June 1855, that Corporal John Lyons performed a life-saving action.

wife and, when young Willy was old enough, a commission was purchased into the 7th Hussars.

When he was 21, he travelled to India with his regiment to take part in quelling the Indian Mutiny. During the second attack on Lucknow in March 1858, Cornet Bankes was attached to a troop escorting some artillery in the country north of the city. They spotted a small mud fort and rode to investigate. Suddenly they were charged by a mob of sword-wielding rebels and were soon involved in a fierce mêlée. Two officers were severely wounded, which left Willy as the only remaining officer. He charged into the crowd, shooting three rebels. Bankes' horse was hamstrung and he was unseated. Powerless to defend himself, he was repeatedly slashed with *tulwars* and knives.

His brother, Edward, witnessed the incident: 'I was on duty with my brother and a shell happened to drop among us. Most of the men, and there were about 20, lay down flat, but my brother had the presence of mind to throw the shell over the parapet … Shortly afterwards to my brother's great surprise, he received £5 from the Commander-in-Chief for his bravery and when he came home the Queen pinned the Victoria Cross on his breast.' He was forced to leave the Army because of chronic rheumatism. He died on 20 April 1867 at the age of 44 in County Kildare. A memento mori was taken, possibly with his uniform and medals painted on.

25

Sir Deighton Probyn VC – Honorary Sikh

ighton Macnaghton Probyn was born in Marylebone, London on 21 January 1833, the son of Captain George Probyn R.N. Commissioned in the 6th Bengal Light Cavalry in 1849, he was appointed adjutant three years later in the newly raised 2nd Punjab Cavalry. He took part in the assault on Delhi, the Second Relief of Lucknow and many fights and skirmishes during the height of the Mutiny. The continuous campaigning with its frequent hand-to-hand fighting caught up with Dighton Probyn and he displayed the symptoms of combat fatigue. On medical advice, he was withdrawn from the campaign and sent home to England.

When he arrived back in England, he received his Cross from the Queen at a parade on Southsea Common on 2 August 1858. The reverse of the suspension bar was inscribed, *Capt. Dighton M. Probyn 2nd Punjab Cavalry.* The centre in the reverse of the Cross, however, is undated as his gallantry covered many different dates.

Now with his health restored, the press noticed that he was cutting a dash in fashionable society attired in his splendid uniform. An old friend remarked: 'He could not help being showy in appearance – nature made him so.'

His new command, familiarly named Probyn's Horse, was in the field again for the campaigns against the troublesome tribes on the North-

Probyn, Deighton.

Probyn, Dighton 1866.

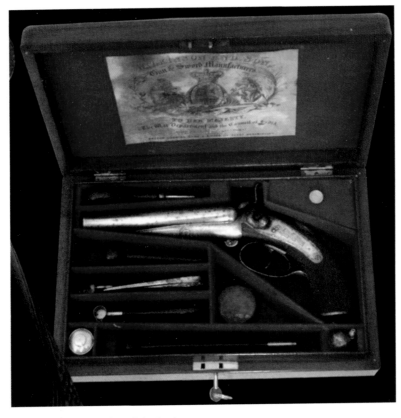

Probyn, Sir Deighton howdah pistol.

West Frontier, including the Umbeyla Campaign of 1863. In 1870, Probyn was promoted to major-general and appointed ADC to the Viceroy, Lord Mayo. Two years later, he returned to England to become equerry to Edward, Prince of Wales and thereafter his life became entirely involved with the Royal Family. In 1877, he was appointed comptroller and treasurer of the Prince of Wales Household, a function he carried out until his death. He accompanied the Prince for his visit to India and was presented with a cased howdah pistol made by Wilkinson.

When King Edward died in 1910, Probyn, at the age of 77, was looking forward to a well-earned retirement. Instead, out of loyalty, he stayed on as comptroller to Queen Alexandra who, if anything, was even more profligate with her finances that the late King. In 1911, Probyn

was paid a unique tribute by being advanced to G.C.B (Knight Grand Cross of the Order the Bath Military Division), becoming the only non-royal to hold this highest grade of the Order.

Probyn began to suffer from gout in his neck, which contracted the muscles so he could not lift up his head or turn it side to side. For his 80th birthday treat Queen Alexandra took him to the Hendon Air Show, but he was so rigid that they had to lay him on the ground so he could see the aeroplanes flying overhead. When he commanded Probyn's Horse he had been made an honorary Sikh and, in deference to this singular honour, never cut his long white beard, which had the effect of covering his VC when he was in uniform. In June 1924, he was taken ill at Sandringham and died in Queen Victoria's room.

26

Edmund Lenon and Pawned VC

While Britain was involved in her wars against the Russians and then her fractious Indian sepoys, another confrontation was brewing in China. In 1858, a treaty had been signed opening up more Chinese ports to European trade but when the British and French ambassadors attempted to sail up the Pei-Ho River to Peking to ratify the treaty, they were fired on by the formidable Taku Forts guarding the waterway.

In 1860, a 17,000 strong Anglo–French force was landed to destroy the Taku Forts and march on Peking. Because of the marshes and the narrow causeway across them, the attacking force was restricted to 2,500 British and 400 French troops.

Attacking at dawn on 21 August 1860, the troops advanced under heavy musket fire until they reached the sun-baked mud walls of the North Fort. Lieutenant Robert Rogers and Private John McDougall of the 44th Regiment, together with Lieutenant Edmund Lenon, 67th Regiment, swam the water-filled ditches and reached the fort. They were followed by Ensign John Chaplin, also of the 67th Regiment, who carried the Queen's Colour of the Regiment. Scaling the wall with the aid of swords thrust into the mud walls, they reached an embrasure. Lenon and McDougall were first in and both received wounds. Once the breach had been made and rest of the attacking force followed, then the battle was all but won.

Lenon, Edmund.

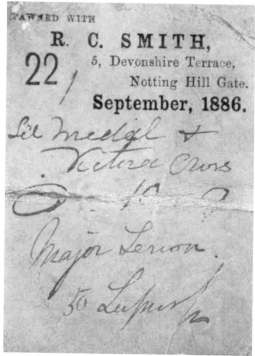

Lenon, pawn ticket.

Lenon, Taku Fort entrance.

A total of seven VCs were won that morning, including Lieutenant Lenon, who received his Cross in Dublin from the GOC Ireland, General Sir George Brown. He married a vicar's daughter, Mary Margaret Morgell, and remained in Ireland before retiring in 1869. He was appointed lieutenant-colonel of the 2nd Volunteer Battalion of the Queen's Own Royal West Kent Regiment, a latter-day territorial force. Lenon took up stock brokering and became involved in a fraud scandal, narrowly avoiding prosecution. In 1878, he ceased trading as a stockbroker and would seem to have financial problems for he pawned his Victoria Cross for the paltry sum of 10 shillings (£56 today). He would have been aware that he could have auctioned his Cross for at least £23 (£1,830), so why did he pawn his VC for so little?

The answer is he indulged in several adulterous affairs, including one with the wife of a fellow officer in the 2nd VB, which would have resulted in his immediate resignation as honorary colonel. Tired of his extra-marital affairs his wife filed for judicial separation. It seems probable that he pawned his VC as a means of hiding it from any legal claims from his wife. In the event, he succumbed to sickness at the age of 54 and died at St Thomas's Hospital in 1893. Twenty years later his VC was auctioned for £125 (£13,500) and bought by the Hampshire Regiment.

27

George Fosbery – Firearms Inventor

George Vincent Fosbery was born at the family seat at Fosbery near Devizes, Wiltshire, on 11 April 1832 to the Reverend T.V. Fosbery. He was educated at Eton and attended Addiscombe College before being commissioned into the Bengal Army on 20 January 1852. He was appointed to 48th Bengal Native Infantry and then 3rd BNI on 18 July 1856. Promoted to lieutenant on 1 July 1857, he arrived just as the events of the Indian Mutiny were unfolding. For some reason he was granted a leave back to England, which lasted until 1861, so missing taking part in the Mutiny. The 3rd BNI mutinied and Fosbery, although absent, was placed on the roll of the 4th Bengal European Regiment.

He would appear to have had an innovative bent more suited to the Ordnance Department. He did volunteer for the Umbeyla Campaign of 1863, one of the many expeditions in the North-West Frontier region, commanding thirty marksmen drawn from Her Majesty's 71st Regiment and 101st Fusiliers who were

Fosbery, G, Webley-Fosbery revolver.

Fosbery, George.

armed with one of his inventions; the explosive bullet. This was developed as a means of ascertaining range distances for the Mountain Artillery and Infantry. He was awarded the

Victoria Cross together with Lieutenant Henry Pitcher in the fierce hand-to-hand fighting for Crag Piquet. This strategic feature fell to the Pashtuns three times in four weeks only for the British forces to retake it on each occasion. Both Fosbery and Pitcher were recommended for the Victoria Cross and, as often happened with recipients who served in India, they received their award by registered post.

George Fosbery served with several Indian regiments, none for very long, before retiring as lieutenant-colonel in 1877. On returning to England, his firearm skills were recognised and he concentrated on his passion for invention. With the advent of the machine gun into the British Army he helped perfect its development. His main claim to fame was the 'Paradox Gun', an automatic revolver that bears his name. Invented in 1895, it was taken up by the Webley & Scott Revolver and Arms Company. The Webley-Fosbery Automatic Revolver was subsequently produced as a six-shot .455 calibre and an eight-shot .38 calibre. About 4,000 were issued in the First World War but, although effective in normal conditions, the mud and muck of the trenches rendered the gun unreliable.

28

Duncan Boyes – The Fallen Hero

Boyes, D, VC medal.

Duncan Gordon Boyes was born in Cheltenham on 5 November 1846 and attended Cheltenham College. He may have been inspired by his new brother-in-law, Thomas Young, who married his sister Louisa Mary in 1860. Lieutenant Young was the gunnery officer on the new steam frigate HMS *Shannon* and had been awarded the Victoria Cross as part of Captain William Peel's Navy Brigade during the Indian Mutiny. Duncan Boyes prepared for a career in the Royal Navy at North Grove House Academy and was appointed Midshipman on HMS *Euryalus*.

Boyes' new ship was part of an international squadron that sought to open the narrow Shimonoseki Straits at the western end of the Japanese Inland Sea. The local Samurai chieftains were opposed to any western influence and committed acts of murder on Europeans and fired on their ships. In retaliation, twenty-eight ships of the international squadron silenced the Japanese batteries and landed to spike the guns. As the crew of *Euryalus* prepared to re-embark, they were attacked by a strong Japanese force that had gathered at the end of a valley behind the battery. Carrying the Queen's Colour was Midshipman Boyes, supported by two colour sergeants, one being Thomas Pride. In the charge towards the Japanese palisade, Boyes was in the forefront holding the colour aloft despite the heavy fire.

At the end of the charge when the enemy had retreated, the flag was found to have six musket ball holes torn in it. One of the colour sergeants had been killed and Thomas Pride severely wounded. For their outstanding gallantry, Boyes, Pride and Ordinary Seaman William Seeley were awarded the Victoria Cross. Queen Victoria was so impressed by the reports that she issued a royal command for large parade to be held on Southsea Common and the VCs to be presented by Admiral Sir Michael Seymour, GOC Portsmouth. Many of the previous naval VCs were in attendance as HMS *Victory* fired a

Boyes, Duncan, Shimonoseki.

Boyes, Duncan.

salute and the large gathering gave three cheers.

Sadly, this was the height of Midshipman Boyes' career for barely two years later he was dismissed from the Royal Navy for what appeared a trifling offence. When stationed in Bermuda, he and another midshipman were caught trying to break into the Navy Yard without a pass. Although there was no talk of taking away his VC, the blow of dismissal caused the youngster to have fits of depression made worse by heavy bouts of drinking. His family decided to send him out to New Zealand, where his elder brothers ran a sheep station in Otago Province. This did little to alleviate the depression and he suffered a nervous breakdown. In Dunedin on 26 January 1869, after a drinking session, he jumped out of an upper-floor window and was killed. This was to be a double blow to his family, and his sister in particular, for Thomas Young died two months later on 20 March 1869.

29

The Mystery of Timothy O'Hea VC

One of the most intriguing of all VCs is the case of Timothy O'Hea. It is significant on two counts; firstly, how he came to be recommended for the Cross despite not being in the presence of an enemy, and, secondly, for the manner of his death.

Timothy O'Hea was born at Schull, County Cork, on 11 June 1843. Like many of his countrymen, poverty forced him to join the British Army. On 6 November 1863, he enlisted in Dublin with the 1st Battalion Rifle Brigade. He was immediately posted to Canada, where the regiment had been sent in 1862 to guard against any threat of invasion from the United States, involved in its Civil War. When this ended another threat was rekindled when a large number of discharged soldiers of Irish descent established the Fenian Brotherhood with the intention of capturing parts of Canada to force the British Government into a trade-off to grant independence to Ireland.

In early June 1866, Private O'Hea was one of four men delegated to escort a boxcar loaded with munitions and blankets to supply the troops on the border. In order that it should be unnoticed by Fenian spies, the boxcar was attached midway to a four-carriage passenger train carrying German immigrants. As the train moved in to the station of the small town of Danville, about 70 miles from the Vermont border, an alert engineer spotted smoke and fire coming from the ammunition car, which contained more than 2,000 rounds of ammunition and ninety-five barrels of gunpowder. It seems probable that sparks from the engine had set alight the dry timbers of the boxcar. Also in the station at the

O'Hea, Timothy.

time were two full passenger trains. O'Hea and the brakeman were the only ones to react and together they put out the fire. His gallantry was noted and a report was sent to Horse Guards where the 'inconvenient precedent', the Warrant signed by Queen Victoria in 1858 extending the Victoria Cross to cases of conspicuous courage in the face of danger *but not before the enemy*, was considered. After much bureaucratic argument, O'Hea was awarded the Victoria Cross. Almost immediately, his health began to suffer and he was discharged with terminal tuberculosis.

He returned to his family in Ireland and died, probably sometime between 1869 and 1870. His younger brother John, a known nationalist, took Timothy's identity and VC and escaped arrest

Timothy O'Hea. His brother John, a nationalist, took Timothy's medal when he died, avoided arrest by moving to Australia.

O'Hea's genuine VC.

by travelling first to New Zealand and then to Australia. He was able to collect Timothy's VC pension despite the records showing a three-year age difference, a different eye colour and height. In 1874, John was persuaded to join an expedition into the Outback to discover the fate of a trans-continental expedition of 1848. Poorly organised, the members of John's party died in Sturt's Stony Desert, Queensland. The newspapers reported his death as that of Timothy O'Hea VC and this became his accepted fate. Photographs show the two brothers wearing the VC and their appearance is quite different.

30

Married to Two VCS

A mong the claims for uniqueness in the history of the Victoria Cross, the one to have the greatest claim must be Eleanor Annie Burmester; she was married to two holders of the Victoria Cross, both medical officers.

Eleanor, known as Daisy, was bought up in Halifax, Nova Scotia, the pretty daughter of German émigrés. She met and fell in love with Valentine McMaster, the regimental surgeon of the 78th Highlanders and recipient of the Victoria Cross. His Indian Mutiny VC recommendation came through the ballot method and was almost a last measure. General Havelock called for recommendations for the Victoria Cross and the only regiment not to forward one was the 78th. When further pressed, they sent in the name of one of their medical officers, Assistant Surgeon Valentine McMaster. An apocryphal story that rings true relates to two private soldiers discussing who they would vote for in a ballot. One said he would vote for the doctor because he was the most likely man to live to wear it. When asked why he thought that, the private replied: Because he takes such f...... good care of hisself!'

In 1869, he was posted with the regiment to Halifax and became involved in the city's social life. He met and married Daisy Burmester in June 1870 and together they produced two children. Tragedy struck when 38-year-old McMaster died on 22 January 1872 from heart disease. He was buried in Belfast City Cemetery, where his widow erected a cross over his grave. Daisy, expecting another child, returned to her family in Halifax to give birth to her second son.

McMaster, Valentine VC.

Daisy Burmester (Eleanor) wife of both men.

Douglas, Campbell Surgeon with 24th Regt. VC.

Two years later Daisy met another surgeon, Canadian-born Campbell Millis Douglas of the Royal Artillery, and married him on 10 August 1874. As an accomplished boatman, he had been awarded the Victoria Cross in 1867 for skilfully handling a small boat crewed by volunteers through heavy surf to rescue seventeen men stranded on a beach in the Andaman Islands. At the time he had been the medical officer of the 24th Regiment based in Burma and sailed to save his stranded comrades from the cannibals who lived on the island.

When he retired from the Army, he returned to Canada and was put in charge of a field hospital during the Riel Rebellion of 1885. At the end of this campaign, he moved back to England with his family, now increased to six. Daisy died in 1894 at the early age of 45 and Douglas followed in 1909, dying at his daughter's home in Somerset.

The Only Female 'VC'

The 104th Bengal Fusiliers were stationed in the Punjab when they became the subject of a unique bestowal of a replica Victoria Cross. The recipient was Elizabeth Webber Harris, who left a brief account of the events that led to her becoming the only unofficial female 'VC' recipient:

'In the year 1869, an awful wave of cholera swept India from Calcutta to Peshawar. The 104th Bengal Fusiliers commanded by (my husband) Col. Webber D. Harris was stationed at Peshawar, and in August of that year it became so violent that one wing of the Regiment was ordered out into camp in the district. I hurried back to Peshawar at the end of August. For about 10 days the cholera seemed less virulent though in one week we lost 13 little children and a few women, suddenly burst out again and on 10 September the Headquarters were ordered into camp.

'The Quarter Master had marked out the camp about 7 miles off, but the sun was high when we got there. I dismounted and went into my tent, when I saw a soldier fall to the ground. I called

Webber-Harris, Elizabeth.

Webber-Harris Gold VC.

my servants; we picked him up and sent for the Doctor. Unhappily we had only one with us, so he was sometime coming. The poor man was in a collapse from cholera, and quite unconscious. While waiting, I got some mustard, tore my handkerchief in half and put on 2 mustard plasters, and the Doctor arriving, he was sent off to hospital, and am thankful to say he eventually recovered.

'That night we lost 27 men, who had to be buried on this ground. Next morning, about 3am we marched to another spot. The men were all very much dispirited and as the Colonel and I were walking in the lines at dusk, he suggested we might have a sing-song, offering prizes to the man who sang the best song. It was hurriedly arranged, and a committee of sergeants formed to adjudge the prizes. At 9pm, we all assembled. The men formed a ring, into the centre of which the man stepped who was to sing. It all went merrily, but the night was so intensely hot that soon after eleven, we adjourned. When I came to the last prize, (they were all money) the poor man who should have received it was not there; he died of cholera.

'Next morning we marched again, and so went until we got to the foot of a hill called Cherat, where the other wing, which happily had only one fatal case since leaving Peshawar, joined us. There we remained till the Doctor considered we were not infectious …'

The Regiment had been most impressed by the Colonel's wife that they had a replica VC made with the following inscription on the back: 'Presented to Mrs Webber Harris by the officers of the 104th Bengal Fusiliers, for her indomitable pluck, during the cholera epidemic of 1869.' General Sir Samuel Browne VC asked if he could present it and commented that they should have used diamonds to pick out 'For Pluck'.

32

Donald Macintyre and the Rescue of Mary Winchester

There was nothing like the abduction of a small British child for the Army to launch a punitive action, which led to a little more pink being added to the Raj. The introduction of the Chinese tea plant to the lowlands of Assam and Dajeeling resulted in the proliferation of more than 100 tea plantations. This was too tempting a target for the warlike Lushai tribes, who occupied the wild mountainous region on the Burmese border. On 23 January 1871, the Lushias went too far when they attacked the Alexandreapur tea plantation in the Cachar area and killed the manager, James Winchester. Furthermore they abducted his illegitimate 6-year old daughter, Mary, which was enough to stir the British into launching a punitive expedition. Fruitless negotiation, distance and remoteness delayed the expedition by nearly a year.

Donald Macintyre was born on 12 September 1831 in Ross-shire, educated at private schools in England and abroad. In 1848, he attended Addiscombe Seminary and received his commission into the Bengal Army on 14 June 1850. He was to be forever associated with the Gurkha regiments and, in 1871, was a major and second-in-command of the 2nd Gurkhas commanded by Colonel Herbert Macpherson,

MacIntyre, Donald.

MARY WINCHESTER, THE CAPTIVE OF THE LOOSHAIS.

Winchester, Mary.

Dr.Brydon painted by E.Butler.

the Indian Mutiny VC. They were part of the column under the command of Brigadier Brownlow that had to hack their way through thick jungle to reach the Lushai chief's fortified stockade at Lal Gnura, fighting off two heavy skirmishes on the way.

They finally reached their target on 4 January 1872. Led by Donald Macintyre, the 2nd Gurkhas charged up the steep and rugged hillside. Macintyre was the first to reach the bamboo stockade, which stood 9ft high. All the time the enemy fired on him with a hail of musket balls, spears and poisoned arrows. Despite this, Macintyre and a Gurkha climbed over the spiked fence and hacked a gap for the rest of the regiment to follow. After a stiff fight, the village was captured.

Colonel Macpherson was so impressed he recommended Macintyre for the Victoria Cross.

Macintyre was promoted to lieutenant-colonel and, in 1876, given command of the 2nd (Prince of Wales' Own) Gurkha Regiment. Mary Winchester was rescued alive, well and quite happy. She had adopted the ways of the tribe and had already lost her native tongue. She was found wearing a blue rag around her loins, smoking a pipe and ordering some small boys about. The Lushai seemed to regard her as if she were some sort of royalty. Mary Winchester returned to her grandparents in Elgin, Scotland. When she grew up, she married and worked as a headmistress in London. She died in 1955 at the age of 90.

Major General Macintyre retired and died at his home at Rosemarkie. He was buried alongside his brother-in-law, Dr William Brydon, the lone survivor of the disastrous retreat from Kabul in 1842. He was the subject of Lady Butler's famous painting entitled *Remnants of an Army*.

33

Reginald Sartorius' Jungle Ride

The next military hot spot was the least-regarded of British processions; the Gold Coast – the original 'White Man's Grave'. Britain barely was able to keep its finger-hold on the few coastal ports while the war-like Ashanti tribes dominated the hinterland and threatened to expel the colonists. The inglorious task of suppressing the Ashanti fell on Major-General Garnet Wolseley, who by careful planning and organisation turned this minor war into a glorious victory, further enhancing his reputation.

He took with him about thirty Special Service officers looking for advancement. One of these was Reginald William Sartorius of the Indian Army. He was taken on to serve in the nascent Gold Coast Constabulary, made up mainly of Nigerian Muslim Hausas. While Wolseley's main force thrust north to the Ashanti capital of Kumasi (Coomassie), John Hawley Glover, the Administrator of Lagos Colony, led his Hausas up the River Volta to approach the capital from the east.

On 17 January, 1874, Sartorius rescued a severely wounded sergeant under heavy fire. As Glover's force had expended much ammunition, they were forced to wait to be replenished. Sartorius was ordered to take 130 men and make the hazardous journey to link up with Wolseley at Kumasi. Soon he was completely cut off from

Sartorius, R, presentation goblet.

Sartorius, Reginald in campaign uniform.

any support and decided to send back some of his men to speed up the advance. All the time the small column was threatened but there was no major confrontation.

When Glover caught up with him, he sent Sartorius with twenty Hausas to cover the remaining 35 miles to Kumasi. Menaced all the way by the Ashanti, Sartorius arrived in the capital to find it empty and Wolseley's force already returning to the coast. Sartorius finally reached Wolseley, who was full of praise for his feat of travelling so far through hostile country. A VC was recommended but the Warrant did not cover Sartorius' perilous trek. Under Wolseley's persuasion, the civil servants bent the

rules and made Sartorius' early action in rescuing the Hausa NCO on 17 January the reason for the award, which seems to have satisfied everyone. Reginald Sartorius received his Cross from the Queen but he knew it was for his ride through the jungles of the Ashanti.

In 1875 he was on the Staff of the Prince of Wales when he toured India. He was presented with an ornate goblet by the Prince that was inscribed 'Captain Sartorius on Return From Comassie (sic) 3rd April 1874.' Reginald had a younger brother, Euston Henry, who was awarded the Victoria Cross in Afghanistan in 1879, making them one of four instances of brothers being awarded the Victoria Cross.

34

George Channer – Hero of Perak

Another Indian Army officer fighting the small and largely unreported colonial wars was George Channer. His improvisation finally secured the Perak area of what was to become Malaya; another splash of pink on the world's atlases. The British involvement with India had caused her to ignore her Crown Colony of The Straits Settlements of Penang, Malacca and Singapore. Perak, which lay between Penang and Malacca, was notorious for lawlessness and piracy until the British stepped in and appointed a hugely unpopular resident administrator. When he was murdered, retribution soon followed. In November 1875, a small force was sent but, after a shambolic assault on a stockade, it was forced to retreat. Three weeks later, order was restored to Upper Perak. The country was now entirely under British control except for the Bukit Putas Pass, where the rebels were secure in their formidable stockade.

George Channer was born in India, the eldest son of eight children. He joined the Indian Army and was captain in the 1st Gurkha Regiment at the time of the Perak uprising. Under the command of Lieutenant-Colonel Bertie Clay, Channer and fifty Gurkhas were sent to reconnoitre the enemy stockade. The jungle was so thick that a reconnaissance was impossible. Changing direction, Channer managed to creep to the rear of the fort and discovered that all twenty-five or more defenders including the sentries were eating a communal meal. Beckoning his men to

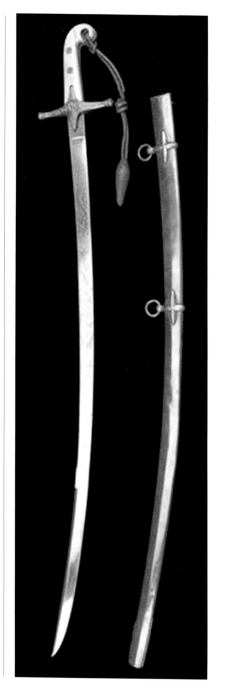

Channer, George mameluke sword.

Channer, George.

join him, Channer clambered over the bamboo palisade and into the stockade. There he saw a log house, with two narrow entrances. Dashing in, he shot dead one of the rebels with his revolver. He was quickly followed by two Gurkhas, who shot and killed two more of the enemy. The rest of the Gurkhas poured in, killing six and chasing off the rest, who made for another log house about 80 yards distant. After firing for half an hour, the rebels retreated from the stockade. On hearing the firing, Clay pushed on up the pass but had to deal with deadly obstacles put in his way. Despite some sepoys firing at the Gurkhas in mistake for the enemy, the operation was a success. Channer lost two Gurkhas killed and two were wounded by enemy ranjons (a collection of sharpened sticks tied together with at least one spike pointing up). This campaign was the first overseas deployment of the Gurkhas and saw the first VC awarded to their captain. Returning to India, George Channer received the VC and was promoted to major. He went on to serve in other campaigns and retired as a full general in 1899. Like many Indian-born officers, he retired to England, where he died in 1905.

35

Teignmouth Melvill and Nevill Coghill – The First Post-Dated Posthumous VCs

Of all the many images that the Zulu War produced, the one that epitomised self-sacrifice and valour for the late-Victorian public was that of Lieutenants Teignmouth Melvill and Nevill Coghill riding together through the Zulu hordes carrying the billowing Queen's Colour to safety from the Isandlwana battlefield.

The reality, although dramatic enough, was somewhat more prosaic. It has never been confirmed that Teignmouth Melvill received any orders to save the colours but he did leave with the flag encased in a cumbersome black leather tube just before the camp was overrun. Nevill Coghill had departed a little earlier and at no time were the two men seen together during the 6-mile retreat along the Fugitive's Trail to the Buffalo River. Here, Coghill managed to coax his mount across to the Natal bank. When he looked back, he saw Melvill clinging to a rock midstream. Coghill was bravely attempting to urge his horse, which had been severely wounded by stab wounds, back into the stream when it was shot dead. Swimming to the rock, Coghill found the exhausted Melvill had lost both his horse and the colours. Somehow they both managed to swim to the shore and begin to climb the steep sides of the canyon. Finally,

Coghill, Nevill VC.

Melvill, Teignmouth VC.

Melvill & Cognill flag Buffalo River.

they could go no more and were surrounded and killed by allies of the Zulus living nearby. Their emotional commander, Colonel Glyn, stated that if they had lived they should have received the Victoria Cross. General Sir Garnet Wolseley, ever critical of officers who he considered to have deserted their men, wrote; 'I am sorry that both of these men were not killed with their men at Isandlwana instead of where they were. I don't like the idea of officers escaping on horseback when their men on foot are killed. Heroes have been made of men like Melvill and Coghill, who, taking advantage of their horses, bolted from the scene of the action to save their lives, it is monstrous making heroes of those who saved or attempted to save their lives by bolting ...'

Wolseley's views did not prevail and Melvill and Coghill remain amongst the most heroic figures of the Victorian era. In 1907, yielding to pressure from the families of the two men, Edward VII granted them posthumous VC awards.

Melvill joined the Army at the late age of 25 and, in 1868, presented the Officers Mess of the 1st Battalion, 24th Regiment, with a silver goblet on his promotion to lieutenant. He was still in the same rank at the age of 37 when he was killed. The Colours were later found in the Buffalo and the Queen granted that a silver wreath should adorn the staff in memory of Melvill and Coghill's gallantry. First World War honours were later added and, in 1934, the colours were laid up in Brecon Cathedral.

36

John Chard – Lord Chelmsford's VC Nominee

The Anglo–Zulu conflict that lasted only six months saw twenty-three Victoria Crosses awarded for a shameful campaign. This is not to suggest that most of the recipients were unworthy of their decoration in any way, but an unhealthy mixture of political agenda and face-saving suggests that the Victoria Cross was not always dispensed in the spirit with which Britain's highest gallantry award had been conceived. On 11 January 1879, Lord Chelmsford led his army across the Buffalo River at Rorke's Drift in the First Invasion of Zululand. Full of confidence, his only concern was that he might not draw the Zulus into battle. He need not have worried, for eleven days later his camp at Isandlwana was overwhelmed, while he led half of his command in a fruitless search for the enemy 12 miles away. Some 1,300 men were slaughtered, including all the officers and

men of the 1/24th Regiment and a good many of the 2/24th.

When he returned to Rorke's Drift, he found that 130 men had held off and inflicted heavy casualties on some 4,000 Zulus. The 2/24th, B Company commander, Lieutenant Gonville Bromhead, submitted six names of his men for the Victoria Cross. Chelmsford sought to divert attention away from the Isandlwana debacle by playing up the role of the defenders of Rorke's Drift. Without consulting the regiment's commanding officer, Colonel Glyn, Chelmsford added the names of Bromhead and Lieutenant John Chard of the Royal Engineers to the list. Chard was the nominal ranking officer during the defence and was probably surprised that he had been recommended for the VC. He may have blasted away with his revolver but it was not clear why he was considered for

Chard VC, Bulldog Revolver.

the Victoria Cross as he was not particularly prominent during the Zulu assault. Those who had actually taken part in the battle recognised that it was Acting Assistant Commissary James Dalton who had been mainly responsible for organising the successful defence. The waspish Sir Garnet Wolseley remarked: 'I presented Major Chard RE with his Victoria Cross: a more uninteresting or more stupid fellow I never saw. Wood (Sir Evelyn) tells me he is a most useless officer, fit for nothing. I hear in the camp that the man who worked hardest at Rorke's Drift was the Commissariat Officer who has not been rewarded at all.' Dalton did receive his VC in 1880. Eleven VCs were awarded for the action; the most for a single action. A newly promoted John Chard returned home and spent several months being fêted, dined and received by the Queen. His subsequent career was unremarkable, but his presence at Rorke's Drift guaranteed his lasting fame.

Chard, John.

37

James Reynolds – Surgeon and Dog-Lover at Rorke's Drift

Many photographs taken of groups of Victorian Army officers inevitably feature a small dog in the foreground. It is rare to find that a dog is depicted in a painting of a battle but this is what Alphonse de Neuville did in his famous painting of the Battle of Rorke's Drift on 22 January 1879.

There is some mystery about the fox terrier as to whether it belonged to Surgeon James Reynolds or was left in his care by an officer of the 24th Regiment, who went to his death at Isandlwana twelve days later. The dog was named variously 'Pip' or 'Dick', although Reynolds referred to him as 'Jack'. Either way, the small terrier stuck to Reynolds' side during the heroic defence as the doctor went around the barricades patching up the wounded and seeing to the more serious cases carried to the storeroom.

James Reynolds, a surgeon in the much-maligned Army Medical Department, was attached to the 24th Regiment, which had a small hospital at Rorke's Drift that housed fifteen patients. It was isolated from the rest of the buildings and became a focal point of the initial attack by the Zulus. Four Victoria Crosses were awarded to the defenders, who managed to evacuate most of the patients as they fought off the Zulus room by room. Reynolds braved the Zulu bullets as he brought ammunition to the defenders and at one point received a bullet through his helmet.

Reynolds was conspicuous among the defenders, moving from one wounded man to

Reynolds, James VC.

the next. One was Private Frederick Hitch VC, who had his shoulder shattered by a Zulu bullet. Reynolds removed thirty-nine pieces of bone and dressed the wound so Hitch could at least distribute ammunition to his comrades. Reynolds and his canine companion were quite unmoved by the shots and spears as they ministered to the wounded. The only time the dog left his master's side was to dash at an over-bold Zulu who climbed the barrier and send him back with a nip in his shins. In the aftermath, some of the defenders paid tribute to terrier that stuck to the doctor's side throughout the fighting.

Jack or Dick, Reynolds', dog at Rorke's Drift.

After much lobbying from the Army Medical Department, James Reynolds' name was added to the list of Victoria Cross recipients. He was further awarded with promotion to surgeon major and retired as a lieutenant-colonel. He kept a photo of 'Jack', which he produced when his grandson asked him about the 'Rorke's Drift dog'. When he died in 1932, Reynolds was the longest-lived of the eleven Rorke's Drift VCs.

38

Henry Lysons & Edmund Fowler – Questionable VCs

The short-lived Zulu War saw a disproportionate number of Victoria Crosses awarded. An unhealthy mixture of political agenda and face-saving, although popular with the British public, did damage the spirit in which the award was given. In some cases it took a fair-minded officer to put forward the name of a deserving other rank to be rewarded who would have been otherwise overlooked, as with the case of Private Samuel Wassall. Conversely, an undeserving officer with a high-ranking parent in Whitehall with the right connections could rigorously push his case for several years before a VC was granted.

This happened in the attack on the Zulu stronghold of Hlobane on 28 March. Led by Colonel Evelyn Wood, the plan was to assault the eastern and western slopes simultaneously; a formidable task as Hlobane was protected by huge masses of boulders and scrub hiding caves and fissures from where the Zulus could ambush the assailants. Wood and his small escort followed the main assault east along the base of the mountain and soon he could

Fowler, E.

Lysons, Henry.

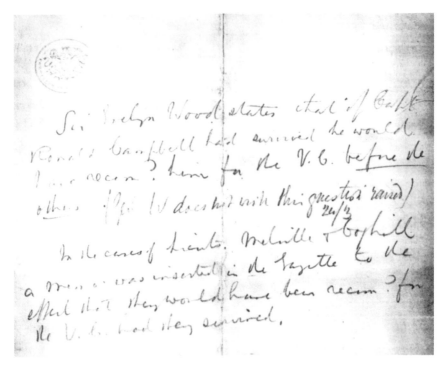

Lysons, VC Document.

hear gunfire as his troops reached the top. As he made his leisurely way in the wake of the attack, his party came under heavy fire from the labyrinth of rockfalls above. Llewellyn Lloyd, a civilian interpreter, was killed and the rest of the party took shelter in a nearby stone cattle kraal. Captain The Honourable Ronald Campbell, Wood's chief of staff, vowed he would 'turn them out'. Charging forward and followed by half a dozen men, he clambered over the jumble of rocks until he came upon a cave from where the shots came. Standing at the entrance, Campbell peered into the blackness only for a marksman to shoot him point-blank in the head. The next two men to arrive at the cave were Lieutenant Henry Lysons and Private Edmund Fowler, who fired ineffectively into the dark recess, but by that time the Zulus had retreated deeper into the cave.

With a fierce battle raging forgotten above him on the plateau, a grief-stricken Wood spent considerable time burying his two staffmen.

Later, the ambitious Wood's grief developed into guilt and he gilded the lily somewhat by declaring that, had the well-connected Campbell lived, he would have recommended him for the Victoria Cross. This statement had the effect of persuading Lysons' father, General Sir Daniel Lysons, quartermaster general at the War Office, to use his influence to obtain the Victoria Cross for his son. After three years of lobbying, and after the Warrant had been amended in 1881 to include acts of bravery performed in the course of duty, Wood finally recommended Lysons. It was felt this would not be even-handed unless Private Fowler was also included. Thus, an act that would, at best, result in a mention in despatches produced two of the most coveted gallantry awards.

Evelyn Wood sought to further obscure his handling of the Hlobane debacle by declaring that 'Lysons VC action was the greatest deed I saw performed in my life'.

39

Anthony Booth – The Hero of Intombi Drift

In an era when an officer's report was the only one that was required, much could be hidden from higher officialdom. This was certainly the case of Sergeant Anthony Booth of the 80th Staffordshire Volunteers and his superior officer, Lieutenant Henry Harward. Booth came from a lace-making family in Nottingham and, in order to escape the remorseless misery of Victorian industry, joined the Army in at the age of 18. He saw service in India, Hong Kong and Perak before arriving in 1877 in the Transvaal, South Africa. With the outbreak of the Zulu War in January 1879, the 80th was stationed at Luneburg on the border of Zululand and Eastern Transvaal, far from the main conflict against the Zulu Army.

Supplies came by wagon train from Derby some 45 miles from Luneburg. About 5 miles from Luneburg, the wagons crossed via a drift or ford over the Intombi River. The incessant rain had swollen the river and only two wagons had made it to the Luneburg bank, leaving sixteen stranded until the river subsided. These were formed in to an inverted 'V' laager but the gaps between them were too far apart. The opinion was that the local natives were friendly and the adverse conditions dictated the formation.

In fact the local Swazi tribe, led by Mblini, was an ally of the Zulus and at dawn on 12 March 800 warriors emerged from the early morning mist and attacked the sleeping camp. On the other bank, Sergeant Booth, alerted by a single gunshot, dressed and buckled on his ammunition belt and peered into the dawn gloom. He saw the natives surge into the camp, killing the slumbering occupants. The thirty-five men on the opposite bank opened fire as some half-naked men managed to swim the river. Lieutenant Harward pulled himself onto his horse and called to his men: 'Fire away, lads.

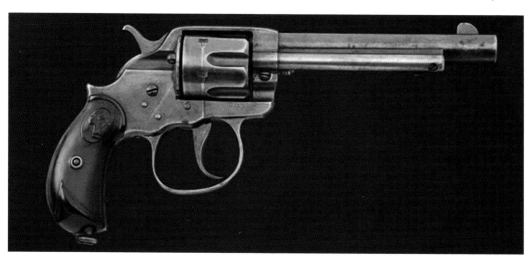

Booth, Anthony. Colt M1878 revolver enhanced.

Booth, Anthony.

Booth quickly organised them into a fighting square and began to withdraw as some of Mblini's warriors had crossed the river. Firing volleys, the small party kept them at bay for a couple of miles until the natives returned to loot the wagons. Meanwhile, Major Tucker at Luneburg led 150 of the regiment to the Intombi in time to see Mblini's warriors drifting back into the hills. In the aftermath, there was considerable covering up for what was an embarrassing episode for the regiment and Tucker particularly praised Harward's efforts in giving covering fire.

By December that year, the 80th was in Pretoria and acting as escort for the new Army Commander, General Sir Garnet Wolseley. Three survivors wrote to him to put the record straight about the Intombi River fight and Wolseley ordered an investigation. Once the truth came out, Harward was forced to resign his commission and Wolseley recommended Booth for the Victoria Cross. In a parade prior to the regiment's return for England, Wolseley presented Colour Sergeant Booth with a Colt M1878 revolver inscribed 'Presented to Colour Sergeant A. Booth VC, by his fellow Officers, for covering the retreat at the Intombi River Drift. March 12th 1879'. Booth received his VC from the Queen on 26 June 1880 at Windsor Castle.

I'll be ready in a minute.' With that he galloped off to Luneburg, where he reported that the camp was overrun and everyone was slaughtered. He was followed by most of his men, leaving a shocked Sergeant Booth with just eight men.

40

Walter Hamilton and the Defence of the Kabul Residency

One the best-known VCs of the mid-Victorian period was Walter Richard Pollock Hamilton. Curiously, he is more famed for his death than the action for which he was awarded his Cross. Irish-born Hamilton chose the Army as a profession and was commissioned in the 70th (Surrey) Regiment. Sent to India, he was then offered a transfer to the elite Queen's Own Corps of Guides, recognised as the finest regiment in the Indian Army. The young lieutenant took part in a couple of punitive expeditions against the fractious Pathans on the wild North-West

Hamilton, Walter statue, NAM.

Frontier. In 1879 the Guides made up part of General Sir Sam Browne's Peshawa Valley Field Force in the invasion of Afghanistan.

In an action at Futehabab, the Guides lost their colonel and the command devolved on Hamilton. He led a cavalry charge at the centre of the enemy, rescuing a fallen sowar (horse-soldier) and distinguishing himself in action. His name was forwarded for a Victoria Cross, but this was declined. A treaty was signed and British troops were withdrawn.

Hamilton, Walter VC.

Hamilton, Walter, printing block with engraving of Kabul action.

The new British Resident, Major Louis Cavagnari, chose Walter Hamilton to command twenty-five Guides cavalry and fifty-two Guides infantry to escort him to his new posting in Kabul and they were given quarters in a compound within the old fortress of Bala Hissar. The already tense atmosphere spilled over into violence when elements of the Afghan Army demanded their back pay, with their anger aimed at Cavagnari. The rebellious Afghans incited the population to rise against the unpopular British-favoured emir and during a spate of rock throwing one of the Guides was fatally struck, resulting in an exchange of gunfire.

The Guides and Cavagnari retreated to the Residency, which was wholly unsuitable for defence. The Afghans brought up two cannon, against which the defenders had no response. Hamilton led out a couple of charges against the gun crews but had no means of spiking the cannon. Two more attempts to capture the guns and pull them into the Residency was met with heavy fire. Finally, the building was set on fire and the survivors retreated to prepare for a last stand. One of the guns blew down a wall that sheltered a wounded Cavagnari and a doctor treating him; both were quickly slaughtered.

Hamilton either made one last attempt to silence the gun or decided to take as many of the attackers as he could with him. Leading a few Guides, he charged amongst the enemy, shooting three with his revolver and cutting down two more with his sword. Finally, he was overwhelmed and hacked to pieces. Hamilton's death put the Horse Guards in a quandary. Having his VC application turned down, they were now presented with another recommendation and one the public were anxious should be awarded. It was decided to bend the rules and change the dates to avoid creating an awkward precedent in giving the decoration after death.

Hamilton is remembered with several memorials and a statue in Dublin. A copy of this statue is now on display at the National Army Museum. The great Imperial poet Sir Henry Newbolt wrote *The Guides at Cabul* to commemorate his death. In the 1970s, M.M. Kaye wrote a best-selling novel, *The Far Pavilions*, in which one of the main characters is based on the archetypal Victorian hero Walter Hamilton.

41

James Collis – Disgraced Hero

Not all VCs led blameless lives but the offences of James Collis, one of the six forfeited VCs, was particularly heinous. In a strange way his crimes lead to King George V famously announcing that: 'Even were a VC to be hanged for murder, he should be allowed to wear his VC on the scaffold.'

Collis was born in Cambridge in 1856 and joined the Army at the age of seventeen. In 1880, he was serving as a Royal Horse Artillery limber gunner in Afghanistan. They were part of General Burrow's force sent from Kandahar to intercept Ayub Khan's 20,000-strong army at Maiwand. Hopelessly outnumbered and outflanked, part of the line gave way and Burrow's small force was overwhelmed. Collis' E Battery waited to the last minute before limbering up and retreating. During the long retreat, with the enemy cavalry harrying them, Collis distinguished himself by saving several wounded and keeping the enemy at a distance with his shooting. These and other acts earned Collis a well-deserved VC, presented to him on 11 July 1881 by General Sir Frederick Roberts VC. There his faultless military career ended.

Leaving the Army, he joined the Bombay Police, married and had three sons. He then re-joined the Army but returned to England without his family. Leaving the Army because of health problems, he was employed as park keeper but was found to be charging couples for acting indecently in the park after dark. He married again, thus committing bigamy. When this came to light, his second wife informed the police. *The Times* of 27 November 1895

A V.C. HERO'S DOWNWARD CAREER.

HE WAS A BRAVE SOLDIER, BUT IS NOW CONVICTED OF DISGRACEFUL CRIMES.

[SUBJECT OF ILLUSTRATION.]

JAMES COLLIS, V.C., thirty-six, labourer, was indicted for indecently assaulting Kathleen Emily Smith, aged twelve, and Mary Evelyn Oxley, aged thirteen, whose parents he was in the habit of visiting.

Mr. A. Hutton, who prosecuted, said that Detective-sergeant Lee, M Division, had made inquiries into the prisoner's past, which had proved to be of a most remarkable nature. Collis served in India as an artilleryman, and at the Battle of Maiwand saved a gun, for which brave deed he received the Victoria Cross. He left the Army after that, for what reason the police had been unable to discover, and then joined the Indian police, but at the expiration of twelve months he gave up his position. Several crimes which he ought to have elucidated remained undetected, and it was suggested that he received money to keep them quiet. He was called upon to explain his conduct, but failed to do so. He then came over to England and joined the Corps of Commissionaires, but was dismissed because he had so many "sisters" visiting him. He was next appointed a constable by the London County Council, but very soon complaints were made with respect to the park under his care. It was alleged that it was the prisoner's practice to allow couples to act indecently in the park, receiving entrance money from them. This was proved by a detective visiting the park one night, accompanied by his sister. The prisoner, at this stage in his extraordinary career, was arrested for bigamy, and at the Old Bailey it was proved that he had married three women, was engaged to a fourth, and seduced a fifth. It was the worst case of bigamy that had ever come before the court. He obtained £50 from one of the women, and when she complained he threw

Collis VC, Illustrated Police News.

THE
ILLUSTRATED POLICE NEWS
SATURDAY, NOVEMBER 20, 1897.

Collis VC, Illustrated Police News.

Collis, James VC.

reported his trial, where it emerged that the VC hero had seduced three women. At the time of his arrest, he was courting another young woman, who had consented to marry him. In another case, he had set up home with a woman and after an argument, had turned her out and sold the house. She bore him a crippled child, which he failed to maintain; damning evidence that the prosecution used to great effect. The prosecution rested its case with the statement that Collis had treated all his women with the greatest cruelty. His lawyer used his VC exploit at Maiwand in his defence, which did reduce his punishment somewhat, but he was sentenced to eighteen months with hard labour.

Collis served his sentence but soon appeared before another court facing a more serious charge of paedophilia. In the *Illustrated Police News* dated 20 November 1897, it was reported: 'James Collis VC, thirty-six, labourer, was indicted for indecently assaulting Kathleen Emily Smith, aged twelve, and Mary Evelyn Oxley, aged thirteen, whose parents he was in the habit of visiting.' The judge sentenced him to two years hard labour. He suffered the further humiliation of forfeiting his VC.

In 1915, he joined the Suffolk Regiment at the advanced age of 58 but died of a heart problem in 1918. James Collis was buried in an unmarked grave, which in 1998 was marked with a Commonwealth War Graves headstone. His sister sent a petition to the King requesting that his name be restored to the register of VCs. Collis and the other five forfeited VCs were restored under Appendix XIII of the Warrant dated 22 May 1920.

42

Israel Harding VC – Quick Thinking Saved the Alexandra

I srael Harding was born in Portsmouth on Trafalgar Day, 21 October, 1833, the son of a master mariner. Inevitably he was destined to join the Royal Navy, which he did at the age of 14. He went on to serve on six vessels until 1882, when he was gunner on the new iron-clad battleship, HMS *Alexandra*. With her 10 and 11" guns, she was one of the most powerful ships in the Royal Navy. She was also the last British battleship to carry her main armaments below decks.

A riot in Alexandria on 11 June 1882 in which several hundred people died, including fifty Europeans, increased the tension. An Anglo–French fleet sailed for the Egyptian port of Alexandria to protect the large European community living there. At the last moment, France decided not to take part, so the British fleet under Admiral Sir Beauchamp Seymour entered the harbour alone. The Egyptian Army had mounted new heavy gun batteries in the forts overlooking Alexandria harbour to threaten the British fleet. Admiral Seymour demanded that the forts surrender within twenty-four hours or they would be shelled.

On 11 July, the *Alexandra* opened fire in a bombardment that lasted all day. She sustained more than sixty hits and one could have proved fatal but for the prompt action of Gunner Israel Harding. He later recalled: 'The *Alexandra* was naturally a special target and there was plenty of her to hit. The excitement began early. A shell came through the port side forward,

Harding, Israel VC.

and bursting close to the sheep-pen, killed the only occupant; another cut away a stout iron stanchion, and narrowly missed the captain and the staff-commander, carried off a piece of the fore funnel casing. Another shell struck the steam launch, and exploding in her, smashed her to atoms, killing one man and wounding two others. Again the captain had a very narrow escape – there were many close shaves that day.

'I was then about to descend the ladder of the next deck leading to the powder magazine when another great shell pierced the ship's side

Harding, Israel. The shell presented the Princess Alexandra.

and passed through the torpedo lieutenant's cabin. It then struck the strong iron combings of the engine-room, and bounded onto the deck among the blue-jackets, who instantly screamed 'A shell! A shell!' I turned round swiftly and saw the awful missile at my feet. I just picked up that shell and flung it into a tub full of water. It was heavy, hot and grimy ... Close at hand at was the hatchway leading to the magazine containing 25 tons of gun powder ...'

Harding was immediately promoted to chief gunner and awarded the Victoria Cross. He was discharged from the Royal Navy in 1885 but volunteered for service in the Great War. At the age of 83, he was serving on a minesweeper when he broke his leg. He died on 22 May 1917, the oldest serving sailor.

43

Arthur Wilson – Torpedo Pioneer

Arthur Knyvet Wilson was born at Swaffham, Norfolk, in 1842, third of six children fathered by Rear Admiral George Knyvet Wilson. Arthur had several naval officers as relatives and ancestors, including Henry Keppel and Horatio Nelson. After just two years' education at Eton, the 13-year-old sat the examination for the Royal Navy and joined HMS *Victory* as a naval cadet on 29 June 1855. Within three months, he was serving aboard the ninety-gun *Algiers* at the bombardment of the Kinburn forts in the Crimea and saw further action during the China War in 1860. He showed a technical bent and in 1870 sat on a committee to investigate a new type of torpedo. Six years later, he became commander of the Vernon torpedo school at Portsmouth and later given command of the new torpedo ship, HMS *Hecla*.

Wilson, Arthur K. VC.

On 12 July 1882, *Hecla* was part of the fleet that bombarded into submission the defences of the Egyptian port of Alexandria. She then resumed her duties in the Mediterranean, which involved frequent visits to the Adriatic port of Fiume. It was here that the favoured torpedo at that time, the Whitehead, was produced at the eponymous inventor's factory. During one of her visits, *Hecla* received orders to collect the marine detachments from the ships of the Mediterranean Fleet and sail for the latest flashpoint – the Sudan.

On 29 February 1884, General Gerald Graham's force advanced inland, adopting a large square formation towards the Dervish stronghold at El Teb. The Naval Brigade was stationed at the two leading corners and *Hecla* had contributed two officers, twenty-five sailors and a Gardiner machine gun. Captain Wilson, who had no role, went along simply as a spectator. When they came under attack from about 10,000 Dervishes, Lieutenant Royds of the Naval Brigade was killed and Wilson volunteered to take his place.

The square was in danger of being penetrated by the fanatical Dervishes and the Gardiner machine gun being overwhelmed. Wilson drew his sword and rushed forward to protect a fallen Marine. He recalled: 'One fellow got close to me and made a dig with his spear at the soldier on my left. He failed to reach him and left his whole side exposed so I had a cool prod at him. He seemed beastly hard and my sword broke

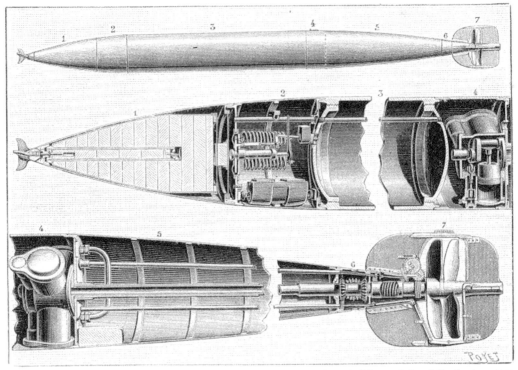

Fig. 1. — Torpille automobile Whitehead. — 1. Magasin. — 2. Chambre à secret. — 3. Réservoir d'air comprimé. — 4. Chambre des moteurs à air comprimé. — 5. Flotteur ou chambre de flottaison. — 6. Mécanisme de commande de rotation des hélices. — 7. Hélices et gouvernails.

Wilson, Arthur VC, Torpedo Whitehead.

against his ribs.' Despite being unarmed, Wilson continued to fight with his fists and sword hilt. A slash to his head caused blood to stream down his face and beard, presenting a fearsome sight. Later he attributed his Victoria Cross to his appearance; 'If only I could have got a basin of water and washed my face I should have escaped notoriety.'

Despite being the foremost authority and champion of the torpedo, Wilson was dead set against its perfect platform – the submarine. In fact, he called it 'a damned un-English weapon' and recommended that captured submarine crews should be hung as pirates. Shortly after attending the Royal Garden Party in 1921, Arthur Wilson died at the age of 79 at his birthplace, Swaffham.

44

Charles Grant – A Tiger in a Fight

The account of Charles Grant's epic VC action in one of the most remote regions of the British Empire reads like a George Henty *Ripping Yarns for Boys*. The death in 1891 of the maharaja of the small hill state of Manipur led to a deadly dispute between his two sons. A palace revolt in Imphal led to the usurper and his followers taking captive the small

Grant, Charles, Inkwell made from 9lb shell.

British delegation and publically beheading five of them. Soon news of this outrage reached the small Burmese border station of Tammu under the command of Lieutenant Charles Grant of the Madras Staff Corps. Mustering a mixture of Punjabi and Gurkha troops, the latter having escaped from Imphal, Grant advanced on the Manipur capital.

Within a few miles of the Imphal, they were forced to take cover in a defensible position at Thoubal, where they were surrounded by some 2,000 soldiers of the Manipuri Army equipped with two artillery pieces and modern rifles. It was from this impossible position that Charles Grant managed to fool his enemy into believing his force was much bigger that it was. He went to the extent of sewing extra stars onto his uniform and referring to himself as 'Colonel Howlett'. He also kept the enemy off balance by leading out small groups in a series of attacks that added to the belief that Thoubal was held by a large force.

After nine days, his men were nearly out of ammunition but still Grant led out his small group of attackers. The following day, the Manipuris, convinced they could not win, retreated. In a later fight, Grant had his horse killed and he was shot through the neck. He wrote to his mother, casually dismissing his bad wound: 'I felt a tremendous blow on the neck and staggered and fell ... feeling the wound with my fingers and being able to speak and feeling no violent flow of blood, I discovered I wasn't dead quite yet, so I reloaded my revolver and got up.' He also retrieved one of the Manipuri artillery shells and had it made into an inkwell, which he presented to his mother.

One of his men said of him afterwards: 'How could we be beaten under Grant? He is a tiger in a fight. When hundreds of Manipuris were coming close, he took 10 Gurkhas out to stop them and in a minute they had driven the enemy back. We could not help winning under such an officer.'

He duly received a well-deserved VC and made a brevet major. This was soon followed by an appointment of ADC to the Commander-in-Chief Madras. He retired as colonel in 1911 but re-enlisted in 1914 with the Royal Scots to serve as a draft conducting officer. He died at his home in Sidmouth, Devon, in 1932, one of the great colonial officers.

Grant, Charles.

45

Randolph Nesbitt's Armoured Wagon

In an action that resembled something out of a Hollywood Western, the bold rescue of besieged civilians by mounted policemen during the 1895 Mashonaland Rebellion was an exceptional feat. On 17 June, Inspector Randolph Nesbitt of the British South African Company Police led seven troopers to a farm in the Mazoe Valley to the west of Salisbury, Rhodesia, but arrived only to bury the dead. They found that the surviving residents had sought shelter at the Alice Mine, whose manager was able to telegraph for help before the line was broken. Seven volunteers rode to the mine through an area full of hostile Mashona tribesmen only to find themselves besieged. Nesbitt had returned to Salisbury and was immediately called upon to lead the twelve remaining troopers to ride to the rescue those beleaguered at the Alice Mine.

Riding through the night, the entered the Mazoe Valley and saw numerous fires burning in the surrounding hills. As they neared the mine they encountered the Mashona, who opened fire, wounding Nesbitt's horse. Digging in their spurs, they galloped out of the ambush and half an hour later found a *kopje* (small hill) where the defenders had formed a defensive laager. Nesbitt quickly summed up the situation. To have stayed and swelled the numbers of

Nesbitt, R. Armoured Wagon.

Nesbitt, Randolph.

defenders would have only prolonged their ultimate defeat, for there was no one left at Salisbury who could come to their rescue. It was decided to immediately return to Salisbury before the Mashona could concentrate their forces. With so many dismounted men and three women, the only means of transport was a wagonette.

In order to make it bullet proof, iron sheets were nailed to the sides. Nesbitt organised his force. He had twelve mounted men, eighteen dismounted and three women but was forced to use six horses to pull the wagon. Volunteers were called to act as the advanced guard, while most of the dismounted men walked beside and behind the wagon. The advance guard were fired upon but, with the whole party arriving, soon drove off the enemy. This was not for long, for the natives kept up an almost continuous fire from the many vantage points along the route. The party were constantly harassed and Nesbitt ordered the advanced guard forward to secure all the higher ground on the line of march to cover the party's advance. Fifteen out of twenty horses were killed, including Nesbitt's. Given the intensity of the fighting, the casualties were light with the party suffering three dead and five wounded, which spoke volumes about the accuracy of the enemy. Given up for dead, Nesbitt's party reached Salisbury to be greeted with relief and enthusiasm. Randolph Nesbitt received his well-deserved Victoria Cross on 12 August 1895.

46

Henry Pennell – First Victim of the Cresta Run

The list of fatalities amongst the sporting officer VCs is sadly long. Heading the list are the horse-riding Victorians and Edwardians, followed by game shooters with their notoriously dangerous hammer guns. There is, however, one sporting death that is unique amongst VCs and it is that of Captain Henry Singleton Pennell.

Born in Dawlish, Devon in 1874, Henry Pennell was commissioned into the 1st Battalion, Derbyshire Regiment. He joined his regiment in India, where it had been stationed since the early 1880s. In September 1897, the battalion was put on alert for active service in response to incursions by the Afghan frontier tribes, which started the Great Frontier Rising. Britain responded by fielding the largest force ever employed on the Frontier. Named the Tirah Field Force, it numbered more than 34,000 men, including the Derbyshire Regiment.

En route, the force passed the Dargai Heights, which had to be taken as there was no alternative route. The Afridi tribesmen were secure in their stone sangers on top of the heights overlooking a bare slope over which the infantry had to cross. A great many casualties had been suffered and the advance stalled. The next to run this deadly gauntlet were the Derbys. First to attempt was Captain Smith, who led out his company, but before he had gone more than a few yards, he fell, shot through the head, and the men immediately

Pennell, H, helmet and tin.

Pennell, Henry VC.

his acute danger, Pennell continued to drag Smith back until he realised that his captain was dead. Placing Smith's helmet over his dead comrade's head, Pennell scrambled back to the cover of the ledge. Henry Pennell was among the four Victoria Crosses that were awarded for this battle.

Pennell went on to serve in the Boer War before entering Staff College. Just after Christmas 1906, Henry took some leave and went for a holiday with a party of fellow officers to St Moritz in the Swiss Alps. Here he was introduced to the pleasures of alpine sports. At that time, British tourists dominated the mountain slopes and are still known as the instigators of the famous Cresta toboggan run. On 19 January 1907, Henry became an unsought first. During a descent, he lost control and went into the difficult bend known as Shuttlecock, where he was hurled over the bank at high speed. It was his wretched luck that instead of landing in soft snow, which the organisers went to great pains to maintain, he landed on a hard and solid mass of ice. His accident was captured by a photographer. The violence of the fall ruptured vital organs, resulting in internal haemorrhaging and he died that night. His body was returned to his birthplace, where he was buried with full military honours.

behind him were mown down. It was then that Henry Pennell performed his heroic but unsuccessful act. Seeing that his captain was no longer with him, he ran back through the heavy fire to try and get him into cover. Smith was a big man and a dead weight for Pennell to lift. Despite

Pennell, Henry, Cresta run accident.

47

Freddy Roberts – The First Posthumous VC

Frederick Hugh Sherston Roberts was the only son of the celebrated Field Marshal Lord Roberts VC, the most revered soldier of his generation. Freddie, as he was known, was described by Thomas Pakenham as 'a delightful fellow; but not very bright, unfortunately. That summer he had failed the Staff College entrance examination by a record margin.' He was lieutenant in The King's Royal Rifle Corps and travelled to South Africa to join them. When he arrived he found that they were among those trapped inside Ladysmith. Instead he was employed as galloper to the commander of the 2nd Infantry Division in its attempt to raise the siege of Ladysmith.

The opening weeks of the Boer War saw the British firmly on the back foot. Disasters at Magersfontein, Modder River and Stormberg were about to be joined by General Redvers Buller's attempt to relieve Ladysmith at Colenso. On 15 December 1899, Buller's force was confronted by well-entrenched Boers on the

Roberts, Fred, with his dog.

Roberts, Freddy. Gun used for his father's funeral.

Ladysmith side of the Tugela River guarding four drifts or fords. Buller had previously given orders to the commander of the artillery, Colonel Charles Long, to site his guns out of range of the Boers and was furious to find that he had ignored this and advanced to within 1,000 yards of the enemy. He was even more alarmed when the guns ceased firing as the crews were swept away by accurate rifle fire. The surviving gunners abandoned the twelve guns and took shelter in a nearby shallow *donga* (ravine).

Buller called for volunteers to try and save the guns and Corporal George Nurse VC and six others stepped forward. To make up two teams, more volunteers were needed and, turning to his own staff, future VCs Captains Harry Schofield, Walter Congreve and Lieutenant Freddie Roberts answered the call. Riding into a hail of fire, both Congreve and Roberts were hit and fell from their horses. Congreve managed to drag the mortally wounded Roberts into the *donga*, where they had to endure a day of scorching sun

and raging thirst. When a truce was called that evening, Roberts was taken to the field hospital at Chieveley, where he lingered for two days before dying.

Buller sent a telegram on 16 December informing Lord Roberts that he had recommended his son for the Victoria Cross. This presented the Awards Committee with a dilemma. Until Freddie Roberts' case, those who paid the ultimate price while carrying out a commendably brave deed carried the citation, 'Would have been awarded the Victoria Cross if they survived.' The combined weight of Lord Roberts and General Buller persuaded the Committee to grant the VC to Freddie Roberts. This opened the door for a further six awards in the Boer War.

An interesting postscript is the gun that Freddie died in trying to save was presented to his father by the War Office. Fourteen years later it was used to carry the old soldier's coffin at his funeral.

48

Two VC Suicides Buried in Same Cemetery

Thirty-six years separated the deaths of two serving VCs stationed at Dover Castle. The reason their deaths are significant is that they committed suicide by gunshot and were buried in the nearby St James Cemetery below the castle. They were also permitted to have a Christian interment by explaining their deaths as accidental.

Charles Wooden was of German extraction and a Sergeant in the 17th Lancers. He took part in the Charge of the Light Brigade, having his horse shot from under him. He was awarded his Victoria Cross when he accompanied Surgeon James Mouat the following day in bringing in the severely wounded Captain William Morris under sporadic fire. Mouat received his VC but Wooden, who was in India, did not hear of this until four years after the event. Horse Guards were reluctant at first but conceded for the sake of fairness that Wooden should receive the VC. He was granted a commission and joined the 6th (Inniskilling) Dragoons as

House, William, funeral 1912.

Wooden, Charles, grave.

Wooden, Charles VC.

quartermaster at the cavalry station at Mhow, India. He transferred to the 5th Lancers and then the 104th Bengal Fusiliers. It was while he was stationed at Dover Castle that the shocking event occurred. On 25 April 1876, Wooden was found in his quarters bleeding profusely from a head wound. A small pocket pistol was found that had been fired twice. He claimed he had a severe toothache and had tried to shoot out the offending tooth. This extreme form of dentistry resulted in the bullet lodging in his brain and he expired that evening. His funeral was an extravagant affair and his fellow officers erected a handsome headstone.

William House came from a farm labouring family near Thatcham, Berkshire. Escaping from this life of poverty, he joined The Royal Berkshire Regiment and fought in the Boer War. Approaching a Boer strong point, he went out under very heavy fire in an attempt to rescue his sergeant but was wounded in the head. He called to his companions not to attempt to help him and he lay in the open until the firing died down. He was awarded the VC and received his Cross from King Edward VII on 24 October 1902. Two years later his time expired but civilian life did not suit him so he re-joined his old regiment. He served in the

House, William, grave.

House, William VC.

Sudan and India, which may have explained his personality change when he returned to Dover Castle. He had become withdrawn and listless, and subject to blinding headaches. Just before 8 am on 28 February 1912, in the presence of six companions, he tied his pull-through lanyard to his bed frame and attached the other end to the trigger. Standing up, he put the muzzle in his mouth and blew his brains out.

Both suicides were aggravated by wounds and excessive heat leading to severe depression. As befitting a hero, William House was given a funeral at St James's Cemetery with full military honours. It was not until 1994 that a Commonwealth headstone was erected by the regiment.

49

Matthew Meiklejohn – One-Armed Hero

orn on 27 November 1870, Matthew Fontaine Maurey Meiklejohn was christened in a singular way by his parents, who named him after the American oceanographer Matthew Fontaine Maurey. After attending the Royal Military College, he was commissioned and posted to India to join the 1st Battalion, Gordon Highlanders. His regiment was part of the 15,000-strong relief force sent to rescue 370 Indian troops and six officers besieged in the small wood and mud fort on the banks of the Chitral River. The Tirah Campaign soon followed, which saw Lieutenant Meiklejohn assaulting the heights at Dagai and taking part in the tough mid-winter fighting in the Bara Valley.

Newly promoted, Captain Meiklejohn stayed in India with the Gordon's 2nd Battalion before being sent to South Africa at the start of the Boer War. Stationed in Ladysmith, he took part in the Battle of Elandslaagte, one of the rare early British victories. During the fighting, Meiklejohn was hit four times in his right arm and lay in pitch darkness and cold torrential rain until he was eventually found. He was taken back to Ladysmith, where his arm was amputated. He lay in hospital for the whole of the Siege of Ladysmith and was lucky not to suffer the ravages of disease and starvation. On 15 December 1900, Captain Matthew Meiklejohn

Meiklejohn memorial Knightsbridge Barracks.

was presented with the Victoria Cross at Windsor Castle. He had the distinction of being the last officer invested by Queen Victoria before her death on 22 January 1901.

Recovering his health, he was appointed garrison adjutant on the island of St Helena, which housed some 5,000 Boer prisoners of war. At the end of hostilities he entered Staff College and in 1911 was promoted to major. Seconded to the General Staff at Army HQ in London, it was in this capacity on 28 June 1913 that he met his untimely death.

He rode a particularly frisky horse that threw him during a parade. Two days later, while he was exercising his mount in Hyde Park, it became unmanageable and bolted. A witness stated that: '[her nanny] and my children were in Hyde Park on Saturday afternoon, 28 June. They had reached a spot opposite to Knightsbridge Barracks, and, as they were walking along the path, Major Meiklejohn on his runaway horse suddenly came upon them between the trees. In order to avoid danger to the children, he turned his horse against the railings of Rotten Row, which he must have known he could not clear. He thus gave his life for theirs, and added one more to the long roll of his brave and unselfish deeds.'

Meiklejohn, M.F.M.

Meiklejohn was badly injured and taken to Middlesex Hospital. After lingering for a week, he died on 4 July. A memorial plaque was later raised at the entrance gates of Hyde Park Cavalry Barracks. It is now sited out of public view within the barracks.

50

Arthur Richardson – Stolen Identity

There will always be those who deceive and claim awards for bravery. Some have the gall to wear the Victoria Cross and, in one incidence, got away with it for ten years. This man was Arthur Henry Leonard Richardson, who assumed the name and VC of Arthur Henry Lindsay Richardson. The latter was born in Southport but after rebelling against his mother's complete control over his life, caught a boat in 1894 and sailed for Canada. There he joined the North West Mounted Police and thrived in his new-found freedom; there was even talk of him being commissioned. When the Boer War started in 1899, an entrepreneur named Donald Alexander Smith, 1st Baron Strathcona and Mount Royal, recruited and equipped a cavalry regiment at his own expense for service in South Africa. Lord Strathcona's Horse, as it was named, drew its skilled recruits mainly from cowboys and members of the NWMP. One of the first to enlist was Arthur Richardson.

On 5 July 1900, Strathcona's Horse was scouting ahead of General Buller's army as they drove the Boers from the Transvaal. As they approached Wolve Spruit they were ambushed by about eighty Boers concealed in a dried up water course. As the Canadians withdrew, Richardson noticed that one of the troopers had been wounded and pinned under his horse. Turning, he spurred his horse through the Boer fire, dragged the wounded man from under his dead horse and pulled him up onto his own mount. Digging in his spurs, he ran the gauntlet of fire until he reached safety. For this action he was the first member of the Canadian Forces to be awarded the VC. A painting of his exploit was commissioned in 1902 and used by the Anheuser-Busch Brewery in the United States to advertise its beers.

Sadly, on his return to Canada fortune took a nosedive and Richardson suffered a series of misfortunes that would dictate the rest of his life. His new wife's health went into a decline and she was diagnosed with tuberculosis, which spread to her spine. The strain of balancing his work and domestic life took its

Richardson, Arthur, anheuser-busch-fine beers.

toll and the family descended into destitution. Finally, Arthur Richardson returned home to Liverpool, where his wife died. He sought employment as a maintenance labourer with the Liverpool Corporation Tramways and for fourteen years worked anonymously on the streets of Liverpool.

Unknown to him, the bogus Arthur Richardson had enlisted in the Gordon Highlanders at the outbreak of the Great War. As a 'VC' he was a welcome volunteer in the regiment's recruitment campaigns. He was promoted to corporal and served throughout the war. After the war, he was feted as a hero and invited to the Royal Garden Party at Buckingham Palace on 26 June 1920. When he died, the truth was revealed and the real Arthur Richardson felt he had to put himself forward. He did attend the Victoria Cross Dinner at the House of Lords in 1929 but continued working as a foreman labourer until his death in 1932.

Richardson, Arthur.

Richardson, Arthur rescue, Boer War.

51

Thomas Crean – VC and International Rugby Player

One of the most charismatic of all VCs must be the Irishman Thomas Crean. As a student he was regarded as a fine athlete and swimmer, and it was using the latter skill that he first demonstrated his bravery. On 11 September 1891, he rescued a young student from the sea and was rewarded by the Royal Humane Society. In October that year he began medical studies at the Royal College of Surgeons and later graduated. Standing 6ft 2in, 16 stone and able to run 100 yards in 10.5 seconds, he was the perfect rugby forward. This was soon recognised for he played for Ireland in the mid-1890s and toured South Africa with an Anglo–Irish squad, a forerunner of the British Lions. He so liked South Africa that he remained behind as his teammates returned home. He worked for a time at the Johannesburg Hospital before opening his own practice.

When the Anglo–Boer War started in 1899, Crean joined the newly raised local Johannesburg regiment, the Imperial Light Horse and, within a month, was fighting at the Battle of Elandslaagte. The regiment withdrew to Ladysmith and was besieged from November to 28 February 1900. On 6 January there was heavy fighting on Wagon Hill to the south-west of Ladysmith, where they eventually drove off the Boers. With so many wounded and an increasing number of sick, Crean and a fellow trooper, who was a qualified doctor, transferred to work in the hospital.

A month after they were freed, Crean rode with 1,100 men to relieve Mafeking, which after several fights was achieved. By the end of 1900, Crean was commissioned but his service as a man of medicine was recognised and he became the regiment's medical officer. At Tygerskloof on the morning of 18 December 1901, the Boers led by De Wet swooped down on what they thought was a supply train, only to find it was the Imperial Light Horse. A fierce fight followed and several Light Horsemen were wounded. Tom Crean ignored the Boer bullets as he went from one to another dressing their wounds. Making such a large target, Crean was shot through the arm, to be followed by what appeared to be a mortal wound to the stomach.

Invalided back to England, he received a telegram from his commander, Major Charles

Crean, Thomas Boer War VC.

Crean, Thomas. Telegram of congratualtions from ILI.

Briggs, congratulating him on the award for the Victoria Cross. Later, he was also commissioned in the Royal Army Medical Corps. In 1905 he married a beautiful Spanish girl and resigned his commission, setting up practice in the fashionable Harley Street in London. When the First World War began in August 1914, Crean's old commander, now General Briggs, in command of the 1st Cavalry Brigade of the British Expeditionary Force, insisted he serve with him. Briggs described Crean as 'the most fearless man I have ever seen'. Life in the trenches eventually took its toll and Surgeon Major Crean was invalided home suffering from diabetes. The deterioration of his health, the sights he had witnessed and mounting debt made his last years sad for him. In 1923, at the age of 49, he died at his London home of diabetes.

52

Ernest Towse – Blinded, He Helped His Fellow Sufferers

Bravery comes in many forms; an act of humanity under enemy fire or routing the foe despite being heavily outnumbered; or, despite a crushing disability, bettering the lives of others. Just one of these examples of gallantry would be enough for the average brave soul. There was, however, one man who could claim to have scaled all these challenges.

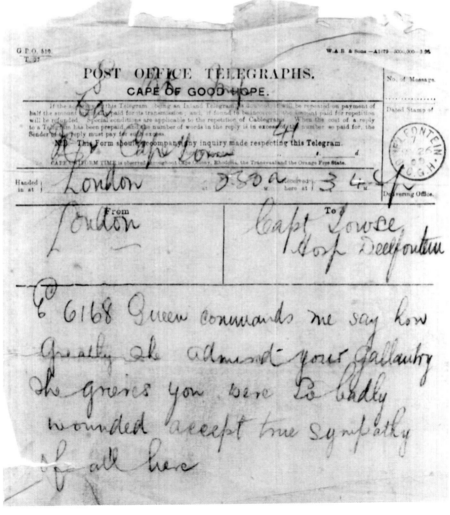

Towse, Ernest, Telegram from Queen.

251/64

                    32 Stationary Hospital.
                         near Wimereux.   B.E.F.   France.
                              16   April.   1917.
Private O.S.Webb.

        I am writing to you at the request of your
Brother, Private B.L.Reed of the 78 Canadians, who is now
an inmate of the above Hospital, suffering from a wound in the
Right Shoulder. He is now going on as well as can be expect-
-ed, and is a good deal easier than he was on admission here.

        He is having every possible care & attention and has
for the moment all that he requires.

        He sends you and his Brother his very best & kindest
remembrances and he is very anxious to hear how you Both are
and how you are getting on. He is likely to be here for a week
or ten days.

        May I al so wish you and those with you, the Very Best of
Good Luck and a Speedy & Safe Return. You have all at the
Front done splendidly, and we are all proud of you.

                    E.B.B.Towse. Captain
                         The Gordon Highlanders

Towse, Ernest, Typical letter he typed in WW1.

Towse, Ernest.

In 1864 Ernest Beachcroft Beckwith Towse was born in London and attended RMA Sandhurst, from where he was commissioned in the Gordon Highlanders. He displayed his endurance when he went elephant hunting in the jungles of Ceylon and became separated from his tracker. He had made one kill and cut off the tail as proof, which was fortuitous as it was the only food he had for three days until he reached safety. He took part in the relief of Chitral, and the attack on the Heights of Dagai. During the Boer War, he stayed with his mortally wounded colonel at the disastrous battle of Magersfontein, which was noted in his VC citation.

On 30 April 1900, he and twelve men confronted about 150 Boers on the summit of Mount Thaba, east of Bloemfontein. Ordered by the Boers to surrender, Towse and his men opened fire. In the ensuing exchange, Towse was shot in the eyes, rendering him blind. Despite being outnumbered, the Boers retreated, leaving the British to secure the hill. The whole action had been witnessed through binoculars by Winston Churchill and Major-General Smith-Dorrien, who recommended Towse for the Victoria Cross. In a private audience, a visibly affected Queen Victoria invested Towse with the Cross and later appointed him as a sergeant-at-arms and a member of the Honourable Corps of Gentlemen-at-Arms.

With the same determination and application he had shown as a serving soldier, he would not let blindness daunt him and declared: 'Blindness can either master a man or a man can master blindness.' In 1901, he joined the National Institute for the Blind and for the next fourteen years taught himself to touch-type and read Braille, becoming expert in both skills. So began his great life's work.

In 1915, Towse persuaded the War Office to allow him to go to the Front in France and Belgium to help wounded soldiers in base hospitals. He was appointed as a staff captain but without pay or allowances. He made brief notes in Braille concerning his patients' wounds and the addresses of next of kin. His memory was exceptional and he remembered each individual case, typing letters to parents, wives and friends, to tell them all about their men. He would work far into the night at his typewriter and rarely snatched more than a few hours' sleep. He received many letters of gratitude from relatives and comrades of the servicemen. He was also Mentioned in Despatches in June 1916 by General Sir Douglas Haig. In 1921, he was appointed chairman of the National Institute for the Blind, and when this exceptional man died in 1948, he had seen the Institute's income increase from £9,700 to £500,000.

53

The VC Recruitment Poster

The beginning of the First World War saw a huge poster campaign extolling the virtues of joining a particular regiment. With the distribution of the early Victoria Crosses in 1914–15, the propaganda posters were shameless in their message that an ordinary citizen could join that elite group of heroes. This also spread to the newspapers who appealed to the non-officer class with a call to join the 'N.C.O's and Men who have won the Victoria Cross'. They then list eleven VCs with an arrow stating: 'There is room for your name on this Roll of Honour.' To emphasis the message, it concluded with: 'These heroes would never have won the Victoria Cross by staying away from the Recruiting Office. They enlisted for their Country's sake, and fought as only brave men do.' In fact, without exception, these VCs were all regular soldiers with the BEF. Nonetheless, it was part of the propaganda effort to fire citizens with a desire to emulate those who had been awarded the Victoria Cross.

Even more targeted were the posters depicting VC heroes such as Michael O'Leary of the Irish Guards who, on 1 February 1915, single-handedly destroyed two machine gun nests and captured ten Germans. At that time

Recruitment poster Albert Jacka.

Recruitment poster.

Recruitment poster.

Recruitment poster.

he was the most acclaimed VC and in July 1915 attracted more than 60,000 to a recruiting rally in Hyde Park.

Another poster displayed Rex Warneford VC in the uniform of the Royal Naval Air Service. He was the first aviator to shoot down a Zeppelin on 7 June 1915 over Ghent, Belgium. The poster, however, was not about joining the Royal Naval Air Service (RNAS) but to come and join the Sportsman's Battalions attached to the Royal Fusiliers. Warneford had first enlisted with the Sportsman's Battalion but, disenchanted, transferred to the Naval Air Service. The organiser of this new group was the redoubtable Mrs Emma Cunliffe-Owen operating out of the Hotel Cecil in London's Strand, who had no compunction in using a former disillusioned

recruit to attract volunteers to her brainchild. The slogan read: 'The Sportsman's Battalion's Recruit Who Wrecked The Zeppilin and Won The VC.'

The Lancashire Fusiliers were a little more subtle. They displayed all their eighteen VCs but with no added comment. One extraordinary attraction they highlighted was that food, clothing and accommodation were free if you joined the Fusiliers.

Another poster from Australia showed the Gallipoli VC Albert Jacka surrounded by men playing all sorts of sports with the message: 'Enlist in The Sportsman's 1000. Play up. Play up and Play the Game.'

By 1916, as the casualties rose, this sort of poster disappeared and the public saw it was no longer a game.

54

Norman Holbrook – The First Submariner VC

In the First World War there were scant opportunities for the Royal Navy to demonstrate its power. It was left to the newest branch of the service to draw first blood. When Turkey sided with Germany in October 1914, the Royal Navy sent its aging – verging on the obsolete – submarines to keep an eye on the western end of the Dardanelles. The monotony of patrolling was broken when a constant movement of vessels was spotted 12 miles up the Straits at Chanak, but to reach this target, a submarine had to negotiate many hazards. The Turks had laid five minefields across the Straits and sited numerous gun batteries and searchlights along the shores. It was noted that the Turks had moored the old battleship *Messoudyeh* below Chanak to protect the minefield.

The Navy chose *B.11* to mount an attack as it had recently been fitted with new batteries. It was commanded by Lieutenant Norman Holbrook, who was delighted to see some action even though the mission was regarded as suicidal. At 3 am on 13 December 1914, *B.11* headed for enemy waters. Fighting against a strong current sweeping down the Straits to the open sea, *B.11* slowly crept forward until Holbrook ordered

Holbrook, Commemorative watch enhanced.

Holbrook, Norman, Submariner.

huge explosion. A great pall of smoke enveloped the ship and she began to roll. Fortunately the ship was in shallow water and most of the crew escaped. Struggling to prevent his tiny craft from being swept ashore by the current, Holbrook gained deep water only to be attacked by a Turkish patrol boat. They had taken a lot out of their battery and also lost the use of the compass. The trip back was tense through the minefields at a speed of just 1½ knots, which saw *B.11* surface from the Dardanelle Straits unscathed at 2.10 pm. They had been submerged for nine hours; a record for a B-Class submarine.

Norman Holbrook was awarded the Victoria Cross and his crew of fifteen each received decorations. There was another thoughtful souvenir of their shared exploit when each crew member received an engraved watch with the words: 'Sunk by B.11. *Messoudyeh*. Dardanelles. Dec.13. 1914.'

Holbrook was further honoured when the Australian town of Germanton, the name deemed to be unpatriotic, renamed itself 'Holbrook'. Norman Holbrook was touched by this gesture and visited the town three times. The town also established a submarine museum, despite being 300 miles from the ocean, and the Australian Navy supplied the decommissioned *Otway* as a permanent memorial to the submarine service.

they submerge to 80ft to avoid the lines of mines above them. Finally he rose to periscope depth and saw the *Messoudyeh* about half a mile away. There was little activity aboard as the 700 crew were eating breakfast below deck.

Allowing for the current, he fired off the starboard torpedo and was rewarded with a

55

Sidney Godley – The Rearguard At Nimy Bridge

When the British Expeditionary Force arrived in France, it was hurried into Belgium to protect the French Army's left flank. One of the regiments that saw early fighting was the 4th Battalion, Royal Fusiliers. Sent just to the north of the mining town of Mons, they were tasked with defending the Mons–Conde Canal. Setting up positions around the Nimy Railway Bridge, they waited for the Germans to attack and at 9.10 am on 23 August 1914 the first shells were fired. The two Vickers machine guns were sited behind bags filled with shingle either side of the railway bridge, which became a focal point of the German attack. Lieutenant Maurice Dease was in charge of the Vickers and was killed after being wounded several times. With all the crews killed or wounded, Private Sidney Godley volunteered to take over a machine gun and held up the Germans for two hours while the regiment withdrew.

Nimy-Bridge.

Nimy Railway Bridge, 1914.

Finally, with ammunition exhausted and the Vickers' water jacket riddled, a much-wounded Godley crawled away and was picked up by a couple of Belgians. He was taken to a dressing station, where he was found to have suffered from twenty-seven wounds, including a bullet in the head. The aid post was soon captured and Godley was held captive for four years.

Godley, Sidney in 1916 as a POW.

Along with the other Fusilier survivors, Lieutenant Frederick Steele reached the hospital in Mons, where he took the time to record the gallantry he had witnessed. He scribbled his witness reports about Maurice Dease and Sidney Godley, which led to the first two VCs of the First World War being awarded. He wrote of Godley: 'In defence of the railway bridge near Nimy 23rd Aug. 1914. This afternoon Pte. Godley of B Coy showed particular heroism in his management of the machine gun: Lieutenant Dease having been severely wounded and each machine gunner in turn shot; I called Pte. Godley to me in the firing line on the bridge and under extremely heavy fire he had to remove three dead bodies and go to a machine gun on the right under a most deadly fire; this he did and not a shot did he fire except as I directed and with the utmost coolness until it was irretrievably damaged and he was shot in the head. He left the firing line under orders to go to the rear.' Steele's foresight in quickly recording the action of Dease and Godley proved providential as he was killed three months later at the First Battle of Ypres.

Godley was sent to Berlin for surgery and skin grafts; his back alone required 150 stitches. When he was fit enough he was transferred to the POW camp at nearby

Döberitz. When it was learned that he been awarded the Victoria Cross, he was invited to dine with the German officers on Christmas day. In December 1918, he was able to walk out of the camp, and made his way to Denmark and on to London.

In the defence of Railway Bridge near NIMY. 23rd Aug 1914. This afternoon Pte GODLEY. of B. Coy shewed particular heroism in his management of the Machine Gun; Lt. Dease having been severely wounded and each machine Gunner in turn shot: I called Pte. Godley to me in the Firing line on the bridge and under an extremely heavy fire he had to remove 3 dead bodies and to to a machine Gun on the right under a most deadly fire: This he did & not a shot did he fire except as I directed & with the utmost Coolness until it was irretrevably damaged or He was shot in the head. He then left the firing line under orders to go to the rear.

23·8·1914   F.W. A. Steele Lt. C. Coy Roy Fus

Godley, VC recommendation by Lt Steele.

56

Edward Bradbury and the Destruction of L Battery

The first few months of the Great War saw little change in tactics and movement from the Boer War. The horse still provided the shock of a charge by the cavalry and the Royal Horse Artillery was able to quickly manoeuvre to fire from an advantageous position. This would all change once the two sides ground to a halt and faced each other through barbed wire across a blasted no-man's-land. One of the last instances of movement from both sides was the incident at the small village of Néry during the retreat from Mons.

Pausing for the night after a long, hot march, elements of the 1st Cavalry Brigade under the command of the aforementioned Brigadier General Charles Briggs bivouacked

at Néry, near Compiègne. Aroused at 3.30 am on 1 September, L Battery RHA watered its horses and hooked them to their traces prior to moving off. Suddenly, out of the early morning mist came a 'ranging' shot that dropped into the battery. Soon the whole field was alive with shrapnel and machine gun bullets. The horses were crazed with panic and many were killed in their traces. Captain Edward Bradbury shouted for volunteers as he raced for the guns, followed by Lieutenants Campbell and Gifford and Sergeant David Nelson. The guns were lined up ready to march facing away from the enemy, which added to the numbers of casualties as they strove to turn the 13-pounders.

The first gun was overturned on a steep bank by the terrified horses. The second had its wheel blown out; the third was disabled by

Bradbury, Edward VC.

Bradbury, Edward, Memorial plaque.

Bradbury, Nery gun.

a direct hit that killed the whole detachment. Three guns were unlimbered and turned to face the enemy, who were firing from a range of only 800 yards. Captain Bradbury took command of one gun but the ammunition was 20 yards away, making it a hazardous but necessary task. Soon Campbell's gun was knocked out by a direct hit but the survivors ran to Bradbury's gun and reinforced the detachment. With two guns returning fire at once they made a tempting target for the German gunners. Soon Gifford's gun was destroyed, which left Bradbury's still-firing gun – one against twelve. This gun bore a charmed life despite the constant stream of casualties. Captain Bradbury kept it in action for more than an hour. The unequal duel continued but as the detachment numbers dwindled and the difficulty in getting the ammunition became greater, the fire became desultory.

As Bradbury attempted to collect more ammunition, a lyddite shell exploded near him and he was mortally wounded. Propping himself against the gun, he continued to issue instructions. When he was carried off he is reported to have said to the commander of the 2nd Dragoon Guards, 'Hullo Colonel, they've hotted up a bit, haven't they?' He was buried in the village communal cemetery.

At the outbreak of war, a new committee had been set up to consider recommendations for the Victoria Cross. Both BSM Dorrell and Sergeant Nelson received theirs promptly but Edward Bradbury was not announced until ten days later. The delay was caused by the belief that still existed that a gallant act could not be awarded with a posthumous VC. This grey area was not resolved until the new Warrant in 1920.

57

Philip Neame – Only VC to Win An Olympic Gold Medal

Many VCs are associated with sporting pursuits and one of the most prominent was Philip Neame, a family member of the Shepherd-Neame brewing company in Faversham, Kent. He was an expert point-to-point jockey and excelled at rifle shooting. He was commissioned in the Royal Engineers in 1908 and soon was secretary of the RE Officer's Rifle and Revolver Club, leading to membership of the Army shooting team.

On 8 October 1914, he arrived in France and was soon involved in the front-line activities of installing barbed wire and demolishing structures that could be used by the Germans. Near Neuvre Chapelle, on 19 December, Lieutenant Neame and a sapper party were sent forward to consolidate some captured positions.

A German counter-attack was under way as they stepped over the many dead and wounded lying at the bottom of the trench. The Germans were using their newly manufactured hand grenades, while the British still improvised with empty jam tins filled with gun cotton and metal scrap. He found only three survivors of the West Yorkshire grenade squad, who said that their jam-tin

Neame, Philip VC.

Neame, 1924 Olympics Gold medal.

grenades could not be ignited as all the special fuses had been used.

Neame quickly summed up the situation and took charge. He knew that the fuse could be lit by holding a match head on its end, which would leave just four seconds before the grenade exploded. Gathering as many jam-tin grenades that were available, Neame began lighting and throwing these crude but destructive bombs at the Germans who were advancing up the trench. For forty-five minutes he held the enemy at bay and inflicted enough casualties for the attack to peter out. Ordered to pull back, he continued to act as a rearguard and helped collect wounded men on the way. For this outstanding action he was awarded the Victoria Cross.

In 1924, Neame was a member of the British Empire Shooting Team that competed in the Paris Olympics. Against the outstanding marksmen of Norway and Sweden, he won the gold medal for the 'running deer' event. Between the wars, he added to his shooting prowess by taking up mountaineering and skiing.

In the Second World War, elevated to lieutenant-general, Philip Neame was captured by the Germans in North Africa and incarcerated in Italy. Along with other senior officers, he escaped and was given shelter in a monastery until he was able to reach Allied lines. In making his escape, he had to leave behind his manuscript of his memoirs. Months later, the chief abbot handed the precious manuscript to the liberating American forces, which eventually reached a relieved Philip Neame.

58

William Mariner's Atonement

The Victorian values still prevailed at the beginning of the war and there was nothing the public liked better than a sinner redeemed. During the war, hundreds of known criminals voluntarily joined the Army and served with great distinction in the field. The list included men who were convicted in all parts of the country and registered at the Criminal Record Office at New Scotland Yard. There were 283 names in the roll of honour of all those criminals who were killed or died of wounds, which was printed and sent to every police station in London.

Among these heroes were two who won the Distinguished Conduct Medal, three the Military Medal and one was awarded the Russian Order of St George. One who was awarded the ultimate accolade for gallantry was a burglar named John William Mariner. He was the illegitimate son of a cotton weaver named Alice Mariner, who later married John Wignall. Mariner took the name Wignall but, when he enlisted in the Army, he reverted to his mother's maiden name. The under-nourished 5ft 3in Mariner joined the 2nd Battalion, King's Royal Rifle Corps, in 1900 and served in India. He was twice court-martialled for striking an officer and using threatening behaviour, resulting in long prison sentences. Discharged in 1909, he embarked on a life of crime, was convicted of breaking and entering and served time in prison in Manchester. As he was in the Reserve, he was given permission to re-join his former battalion at the outbreak of war and fought at the First Battle of Ypres.

The following year the regiment was holding the line on the Cuinchy/Cambrin sector close to where the battle of Festubert was being fought. On the night of 22 May 1915, a violent thunderstorm forced both sides to seek shelter in their respective trenches. An enemy machine gun had caused several casualties to working parties and Mariner approached his sergeant to volunteer to go and silence it. Taking a young soldier with him, they crawled through the downpour to the German wire, where the youngster cut an opening. Dismissing him, Mariner, festooned

Mariner VC medal, found in sideboard at auction.

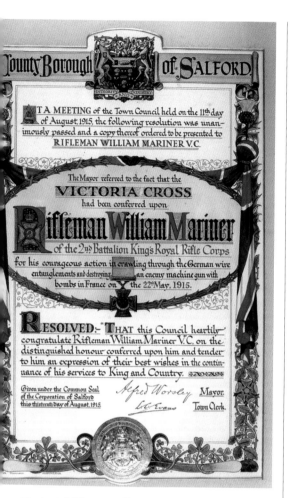

Mariner, William, scroll.

In the British trench they heard the sound of approaching German voices and prepared for a counter-attack. Instead, it was William Mariner returning with two enemy prisoners and part of the destroyed machine gun. For this daring exploit he was awarded the Victoria Cross and his home town of Salford presented him with a watch and an illuminated scroll of honour. His new-found heroic status was short-lived for he was blown to pieces by a shell at Loos on 30 June 1916 and his body was never found. In 2006, his VC was found in a chest of drawers during a house clearance.

Mariner, William, VC.

with two Mills bomb bandoliers, crawled to the enemy parapet. He hurled grenade after grenade into the trench, causing many casualties. He particularly aimed at the enemy machine gun hidden under the roof on a gun emplacement. He changed positions and paused for ten minutes. As the Germans returned to the trench, Mariner continued his bombing with great effect.

59

William Rhodes-Moorhouse – The First Air VC

A long with British aviation pioneers such as John Moore-Brabazon and Tommy Sopwith, 21-year-old William Barnard Moorhouse, who gained his pilot's certificate in 1909, could count himself amongst their number. Born into a wealthy family, his father was a prominent New Zealand businessman and politician and his mother inherited great wealth from the sheep-rearing Rhodes family. William's passion was speed and he travelled to the United States, where he won prizes in a wide variety of aerial meetings and races. He capped his visit by becoming the first man to fly beneath the Golden Gate Bridge in San Francisco.

He joined forces with James Radley and they co-designed the Radley-Moorhouse monoplane, which entered competitions around London. He married in 1912 and one of his presents was a silver model of the monoplane. He made the first aerial crossing of the English Channel with a pair of passengers, one of whom was his new bride. To make the year complete, he inherited a considerable fortune with the proviso that he take the additional name of Rhodes and he used some of the inheritance to buy Parnham House in Dorset. On 24 August 1914, he was commissioned and joined the Royal Flying Corps but was stopped from flying because he had lost his teeth in an accident.

Finally, the growing shortage of experienced pilots over the Western Front brought a posting to No.2 Squadron at Merville equipped with the Royal Aircraft Factory BE.2 two-seat biplane. The Second Battle of Ypres on 22 April 1915

Rhodes-Moorhouse William.

saw the Germans advance behind the release of poison gas. It was a critical time as the Germans were reinforcing their line with reserves arriving by train to the towns of Roubaix, Tourcoing and Courtrai. On 26 April, the RFC was ordered to bomb the enemy's railway network to interrupt the reinforcements. Rhodes-Moorhouse was instructed to attack the railway junction at Courtrai. Flying without an observer to lighten the load, a 100lb bomb was attached to the fuselage. Taking off at 3.05 pm, William had been instructed to release his bomb just below

Moorhouse, grave Parnham House.

cloud level to ensure his safety. Instead, after the thirty-five-minute flight, he chose to attack at 300ft. He was greeted with volley of rifle fire from the troops below as well as a machine gun sited in the bell tower of a nearby church. William was hit in the thigh and the plane was riddled by the heavy ground fire. He managed to drop his bomb plumb on the junction but had to make the return journey under fire again. He received a mortal wound to his stomach but, at 4.12 pm, managed to bring his aircraft back to base; his aircraft had been hit ninety-five times. Despite his terrible wounds, he insisted in delivering his report before being moved to a casualty clearing station.

Just before 1 pm the following day, he received Holy Communion from Padre Christopher Chavasse, the brother of Noel Chavasse VC and Bar. William was informed that he had been recommended for the DSO, but his flight commander lobbied for the Victoria Cross and this granted on 22 May 1915. William Rhodes-Moorhouse's body was returned to his home at Parnham and he was buried on a hillside on the estate.

Moorhouse, Radley-model of their machine.

60

Eric Robinson – Possible Winner of a Double VC

The First World War gave scant opportunities for a Royal Navy officer to perform outstanding acts of gallantry. The exceptions were the submariners and Q-Boat crews but the surface-serving officers got little chance to show their mettle. Eric Gascoigne Robinson proved to be an exception to this rule. He came from a naval family and chose to follow the family tradition. As a midshipman he was posted to the cruiser *Endymion* and travelled to China in time for the Boxer Uprising in 1900. He took part in many battles on the way to relieve the besieged Legations in Peking and his performance was rewarded with promotion. Pre-1914, he attended the training school HMS *Vernon* and became well-versed in the use of torpedoes, mines and explosives.

Now a lieutenant-commander, he served briefly with the Channel Fleet before his elderly battleship, HMS *Vengeance*, along with other capital ships of similar vintage, was sent to force its way into the Black Sea and knock Turkey out of the war. The entrance to the Dardanelles Strait was about 3 miles in width and guarded by artillery and torpedoes. These had to be eliminated before the lumbering Eastern Mediterranean Squadron could affect an entrance. Covered by the guns of the old battleships, Eric Robinson led a demolition party ashore to destroy any serviceable guns in the vicinity of Kum Kale and Orkanieh, an area renowned as being the location of Troy. One of Robinson's first targets was the two guns on top of a hill known as

Robinson, Eric Cmdr with VC ribbon 1916.

Achilles Mound. Plainly visible from the ships in his white tropical uniform, Robinson went from one emplacement to the next, laying gun cotton and blowing up the Turkish batteries. It was only when the Turks sent in strong units that

Robinson, Eric, wounded at Gallipoli.

Robinson, Eric. Star with crown to Order St Anna.

the naval landing party returned to their ships and a recommendation for the Victoria Cross was strongly considered. Soon after, Robinson was involved in commanding one of several converted trawlers for dangerous mine-sweeping operations in the Dardanelles. During the course of this operation, his unarmoured vessel was hit eighty-four times by the Turkish shore batteries.

On the night of 18/19 April, Robinson was chosen to lead a mission to destroy the Royal Navy's submarine *E.15*, which had run aground under the Turkish guns at Fort Dardanus. Using two steam-driven picket boats and carrying a torpedo each, the *E.15* was wrecked. In doing so, one of the picket boats was hit and, under the glare of searchlights, Robinson rescued the crew.

It was now decided to involve the Army and newly promoted Commander Robinson was appointed naval transport officer at Anzac Bay before being sent to the landings at Suvla Bay. Here he was badly wounded and returned to England, where he was decorated with the Victoria Cross. The feeling was that he deserved the bar to go with it. In 1919, he was involved in the naval operations in the Caspian Sea during the Russian Civil War, for which he was awarded the Order of St Anne, one of the last Tsarist decorations before the Bolsheviks overcame the White Russians. He retired as a rear admiral before offering his services in the Second World War as a convoy commodore. He died at Haslar Naval Hospital in 1965 and was buried at Langrish, Hampshire.

61

Herbert James – A Lonely and Tragic Death

Birmingham-born Herbert James was one of those sons whose future was dictated by his father. According to his sister, it was decided he should become a teacher and by the age of 20 he was teaching at local schools but he had a sense that this was not the life he wanted. In 1909, he enlisted in the 21st Lancers, much against his father's wishes. He served in Egypt and India with a view of entering the Civil Service after his service days. At the start of the First World War, he was offered a commission in the 4th Battalion, Worcestershire Regiment, and returned to England. On 25 April 1915, his regiment landed at W Beach on the Gallipoli Peninsula. During the fierce fighting, James was severely wounded in the head, one of the first casualties of that doomed campaign.

Once he had recovered, he joined his regiment in the Helles sector. On 28 June the Lowland Scots of the 156th Brigade sought to push the Turks out of Gully Ridge but mounting casualties stalled the attack. The Worcesters were in reserve with Second Lieutenant James acting as liaison with the Royal Scots. He found that all the officers were either killed or wounded and the Scottish soldiers demoralised. Gathering them together, James mounted another attack and carried a section of the Turkish line. A fierce counter-attack pushed the Scots back and they were swapped with another brigade. On 2 July, James, with his knowledge of the ground, led

James, Herbert investiture.

a detachment to enter the Turkish saps, largely unoccupied trenches used as listening posts. From there they charged the Turks and began to advance along trenches clogged with dead bodies from the previous attack. The two sides began hurling bombs at each other until James found he had only three men left. Finally, with all his men dead, he withdrew along the trench, having sent his NCO back for reinforcements. Armed with a bag of bombs and two rifles, James managed to hold off the Turks until reinforcements arrived. It was a miracle that James emerged largely unscathed and he was recommended for the Victoria Cross.

On 7 August, he went out alone into no-man's-land and brought in two wounded men.

On the night of 27/28 September, he was badly wounded in the foot and returned to England, where he joined the 1st Battalion. He received his VC on 15 January 1916 before taking part in the Battle of the Somme that summer. The wounds he received at Contalmaison necessitated a silver plate being inserted in his head. He also married that year and received a handsome silver salver from his brother officers. He further received the Military Cross in 1917 and a brace of Mentioned in Despatches.

As with so many others servicemen, the effects of the war changed his demeanour. He remained in the Army until ill-health caused his resignation in 1930. His marriage broke up in 1927 and he remarried in 1929. Probably as a result of his head wound, he was described as a shy, withdrawn man with few friends. His second marriage ended in the 1950s and he seems to have become a virtual recluse, buying and selling paintings. He was living in a rented bedsit in Kensington and his landlord later said that he 'was a troubled sleeper'. His solitary behaviour was not noticed until his door was forced open and he was found in a poor state. He had collapsed with a heart attack six days before and had lain on the floor since then. He was taken to hospital, where he died a lonely and forgotten hero.

James, Herbert VC, silver salver.

62

William Williams – Hero of V Beach

Leading Seaman William Charles Williams was described by his captain, Edward Unwin, as 'the bravest sailor he ever knew'. William, named after his gardener father, was part of a large brood including six sisters living in the town of Chepstow. It was small wonder that at the age of 15 he enlisted for Boy's Service in the Royal Navy. After three years' service as a boy he signed a twelve-year engagement on his 18th birthday. He served on HMS *Terrible* and was one of the 267 men who were part of the Naval Brigade in the Relief of Ladysmith. Once this had been achieved, *Terrible* sailed for China to help relieve the besieged Legations at Peking. Thus the young William Williams became one of the few to wear medals denoting Relief of Ladysmith and Peking. For both campaigns, he was recommended for bravery.

When his service expired in 1910, he lived with his sister in Newport and served as a policeman with the Monmouthshire Constabulary. In 1914, he was recalled from the Special Fleet Reserve and joined the former torpedo ship *Hazard*, now converted to minesweeper. His new captain was Commander Edward Unwin who, with fellow crew members

Midshipman George Drewry and Able Seaman George Samson, were destined to be VC recipients. Sent as part of the Eastern Mediterranean Fleet, Unwin was a member of the planning team discussing the landing by British and French troops on the Gallipoli Peninsula. He came up with the idea of using a converted merchant ship that could land more than 2,000 men in one go, rather than from a series of small boats. The ship chosen was the former collier, the SS *River Clyde*.

On 25 April 1915, the converted collier was run onto V Beach and the three lighters were decked over so that they acted as a bridge for the

Williams, William Charles, medallion.

Williams, William VC, Memorial Chepstow.

Williams, William Charles.

troops to get ashore. As so often with such plans there is always a glitch. In this case, *River Clyde* grounded short of the beach. Volunteers were called to pull and steady the lighters while the Royal Munster Fusiliers poured ashore. Williams and Unwin leapt into the water and grabbed the tow rope. With the water around them churned with bullets and shells, the two men held fast for an hour in the freezing water. Their charmed life could not last and Williams gave a gasp and slumped in the water. Unwin caught hold of him but Williams died in his arms.

Six men were awarded the Victoria Cross, including one to William Williams, the first posthumous award to a member of the Royal Navy. On 21 January 1919, a letter was sent to William's sister informing her that a 'Liverpool ship owner' had commissioned a specially struck medallion to those six seamen on the *River Clyde* who had won the Victoria Cross and it would be presented to her on her brother's behalf. He was further honoured by Chepstow when a gun from a German submarine was unveiled by his sister as a memorial to the town's VC hero.

63

Charles Doughty-Wylie – The Middle-Aged Romantic

Charles Doughty-Wylie was a soldier whose later life was taken up with diplomacy and romantic problems. He came from a wealthy and distinguished Suffolk family that included an uncle who was a noted Arabian traveller and writer. Born Charles Doughty 1868, he followed the conventional path to the Army – Winchester and the RMA Sandhurst – before being commissioned in the Royal Welsh Fusiliers. He took part in the North-West Frontier campaigns of the 1890s and served in the Nile Expedition. He fought in the Boer War, China and Somaliland in the 1900s before taking the appointment of British Vice-Consul in Meryna and Konieh in Turkey with its large Christian Armenian population. He also married a widow named Lillian Wylie and changed his name to Doughty-Wylie. It was around 1907 that he met an extraordinary woman named Gertrude Bell, who was working with an archaeologist in excavating the site at Binbirkilise in southern Turkey. Her extensive travels throughout Arabia and Mesopotamia led an amassing of a great store of knowledge and contacts. This was spiced with danger as there was always the threat from marauding robbers, which necessitated her to carry a service revolver beneath her skirts.

In 1908, a group of officers known as the Young Turks began a revolution against the

Doughty-Wylie, Charles.

Bell, Gertrude.

Sultan to reform the ailing Ottoman Empire. During this period of unrest, the Turks began to massacre the Armenians and Doughty-Wylie intervened to save as many as he could with the help of some Turkish troops and the men from the British destroyer, HMS *Swiftsure*. Gertrude Bell was full of admiration of Charles's handling of this ugly episode and so began their ever-closer relationship.

Recently a cache of correspondence between the two middle-aged lovers reveals a passionate but unconsummated affair. Lillian suspected an illicit liaison and warned Charles that she would kill herself if he left her. Gertrude also issued an ultimatum threatening suicide he did not leave his wife. She urged him to ignore the social disgrace of divorce: 'It's that or nothing. I can't live without you.' Doughty-Wylie was in an emotional dilemma but the intervention of the war concentrated his mind.

Employed on the Intelligence Staff for the Gallipoli landings, Lieutenant-Colonel Charles Doughty-Wylie was on V Beach when the attack stalled with horrific casualties. On the morning of 26 April 1915, Charles, along with Captain Garth Walford, organised the survivors from the previous day's fighting and attacked the village of Sedd-El-Bahr and Hill 141. Charles would not carry arms against the Turks, who he greatly admired and having spent much time among them. Instead, waving a walking stick, he led his scratch force to victory. As he stood on the summit of Hill 141, he was killed with a shot to the head and buried where he fell. Both Walford and Doughty-Wylie were awarded posthumous Victoria Crosses; the latter being the highest-ranking officer in the Gallipoli Campaign.

Doughty-Wylie, stained glass window St Peter's Church, Theberton.

Towards the end of 1915, a black-veiled woman visited Gallipoli, landed at V Beach and laid a wreath on Charles's grave before sailing away. Was she Lillian or Gertrude? The mystery remains.

64

Frederick Potts – The Shovel VC

One of the most selfless rescue acts of the First World War must be that performed by Reading-born Frederick William Owen Potts on the scrubby slopes of an enemy-held hill on the remote Turkish peninsula of Gallipoli. In 1912, Potts joined the Berkshire Yeomanry and the following year he displayed his bravery when he saved a 5-year-old boy named Charles Rex from drowning in the Thames. Rex went on to live another eighty-four years thanks to Potts' actions.

The Berkshire Yeomanry arrived on the beach of Suvla Bay on 18 August 1915 and three days later took part in the attack on Hill 70 or, as it was more familiarly called, Scimitar Hill. Potts recalled: 'We were now in the thick of the awful country which I was to know so well. The surface was all sand and shrubs … like our holly trees

Potts shaking hands with his Enniskillin Fusilier rescuer.

Potts, Hill 70 and shovel.

though the leaves were far more prickly … The heat was fearful.' The artillery set the shrubs on fire and many of the wounded perished where they lay.

Trooper Potts joined the final charge on the Turkish trenches but had not gone 25 yards when he was hit in the top of his left thigh and landed in the brush, which gave him some protection. When the Turks counter-attacked, the Yeomanry survivors retreated from the hill, leaving Potts and another badly wounded comrade, Arthur Andrews, to shelter from the Turkish fire that peppered the ground around them. They suffered terribly from the heat and lack of water until nightfall, when they managed to crawl about 300 yards by dawn. They found some water on their dead comrades and spent another day sheltering from the Turks. That night they attempted to crawl towards the British lines but Potts' companion was unable to move far. Potts recalled: 'There seemed no earthly hope of escape when … a way was revealed. Just near us was an ordinary entrenching shovel … I crawled up and got hold of it and before I knew what was happening Andrews was resting on it and I was doing my best to pull him out of danger.'

Despite his exhaustion, Potts managed to drag Andrews on the blade of the shovel for three painful hours down the hillside until they were challenged by a British sentry. The two men were carried into the trenches of the Enniskillen Fusiliers and when the full story was learned, Potts was recommended for the Victoria Cross. When he died in 1943, among the mourners was his companion, Arthur Andrews, who lived until he was 89. A magnificent statue of the Frederick Potts' rescue was unveiled in Reading in 2016.

65

George Peachment – The Under-Aged VC

There were plenty of young men willing to enlist at the beginning of the war, whether for reasons of escaping a miserable childhood or a sense of adventure. One such was George Stanley Peachment from Bury in Lancashire. At the age of 17 years and 11 months, he donned his father's bowler hat and falsely gave his age as 19 years and 1 month as he enlisted in the 2nd Battalion, King's Royal Rifle Corps. After brief training, he was sent

Peachment, Brass plaque.

Peachment, George portrait.

to France as part of the 2nd Brigade, The 1st Division in the ill-fated Battle of Loos. This area north of Lens was a depressingly bleak spot; flat, with German-occupied slag heaps from the many coalmines.

The battle began on 25 September 1915 with the release of chlorine gas by the British, behind which it was intended the infantry would advance and sweep aside German resistance. Instead, a sudden change of wind direction blew the gas back into the faces of the attacking troops. All thoughts of catching the enemy unawares disappeared as the British stumbled on, most disabled by the gas. Peachment, along with some comrades, managed to reach the German wire, only to find it unbroken. The attack petered out

as the men sought shelter in shell holes before pulling back. George Peachment had been made an orderly by his company commander, Captain Guy Dubs. Looking around, he spotted his officer lying wounded about 15 yards from the German lines.

Whether it was a young man's devotion to a kindly officer or helping a father figure can only be guessed but, ignoring the bullets and shells, Peachment dashed to his officer's side and attempted to bind his wound. This made the youngster a sitting target. Within moments a bomb landed close by, driving steel fragments into his chest. Their roles reversed, Dubs received a bullet in the chest as he attempted to move his saviour to a shell hole. Due to the constant movement of both sides and the heavy shelling, George Peachment's body was never found.

Captain Dubs survived the war and later won the Military Cross. He felt a great responsibility for the death of his young orderly and sent a long and moving letter to Peachment's mother in which he wrote: 'I tried to drag him into the shell hole but at that moment a bullet hit him in the head and killed him. I lay beside him there all day and eventually we were picked up when the trench was taken by a flank attack. I can't tell you how much I admired your son's bravery. He lost his life in trying to help me and no man could have been braver than he was … I have recommended him for the Victoria Cross.'

A handsome plaque was installed at the Methodist church that George attended but it ended up in a store at the local museum. In 2006, it was discovered and was ceremoniously inaugurated at St Anne's Church, Bury.

66

Richard Bell-Davies – Return and Rescue VC

Londonn-born Richard Bell-Davies was orphaned at the age of 6 and brought up by his maternal uncle. He was very keen to join the Royal Navy and entered the Royal Navy College at Dartmouth. In 1901 he was commissioned and in 1909 was a lieutenant serving on HMS *Swiftsure*, an unhappy ship due to the overbearing bullying of her commander.

Bell-Davies, the ketch Marjorie.

It became involved in preventing the Turkish massacre of Armenians, providing some protection under the direction of the British consul, Charles Doughty-Wylie, the future Gallipoli VC.

In 1911, Bell-Davies became interested in aviation and received his Aero Club certificate. He was appointed to the Naval Flying School at Eastchurch and by early 1914 was graded as squadron commander in the RNAS. The early months of the war were spent bombing Zeppelin sheds and attacking German submarines at Zeebrugge. In April 1915, the RNAS was sent to the island of Tenados to take part in the Gallipoli Campaign. As an ally of Germany, Turkey received its supplies via the railway that passed through its fellow ally, Bulgaria, and the RNAS was given the job of bombing this vital supply route. Five new Nieuport 12s had been sent out and Bell-Davies managed to secure one. They had been modified to single-seaters by blocking the front cockpit in order to carry 100lb bombs.

On 19 November 1915, five assorted aircraft took off from Tenados to bomb the bridge and junction at Ferrijik on the Bulgarian border. Bell-Davies completed his bombing run and as he turned away he spotted Lieutenant Gilbert Smylie's Farman on the ground about a mile away. The Farman's engine had simply stopped and the only place to land was in the nearby marsh. Bell-Davies saw that a party of Bulgarian soldiers were approaching through the reeds of the sun-dried marsh. While Bell-Davies circled looking for a suitable place to land, Smylie fired his pistol at the downed plane's petrol tank. As Bell-Davies made to land on a dried river bed there was an enormous roar as the Farman's bomb, which had not been released, exploded.

Bell-Davies set his aircraft down on the uneven hard-baked river bed. Smylie ran to meet him and helped turn the aircraft around. The problem was how to carry away an additional passenger. Bell Davies recalled: 'He had to climb over me, slide under the cowl and crouch on all fours between the rudder bar and the engine bearers with his head bumping on the oil tank. He managed to somehow to stow himself away looking most uncomfortable. By this time enemy troops were coming close so I lost no time in taking off. There was length in the dry watercourse for a good run and we had no difficulty in getting airborne.'

This daring rescue resulted in a DSO for Smylie and the Victoria Cross for Bell-Davies. Post-war, Bell-Davies became involved in trials to determine the best way for landing and taking off carriers and it is largely thanks to him that the Fleet Air Arm came into existence. When he retired, he purchased the pre-war brig *Marjorie*, refitted her and enjoyed many years sailing her. Today, she is still sailed by his descendants.

Bell-Davies, R with dog 1915.

67

William McFadzean – An Outstanding Example of Self-Sacrifice

The first fatality on the first day of the Battle of the Somme was a 21-year-old Ulsterman named William Frederick McFadzean. He was a strapping six-footer who played a high standard of rugby in Belfast and was a natural choice as a bomber in the coming battle. He was fiercely Protestant and had joined the Young Citizens Volunteers in 1912 to resist Home Rule being pressed by the British Government. This highly dangerous situation was diffused with the outbreak of the war and Billy McFadzean joined the Royal Irish Rifles. At 7 am on 1 July 1916, he and his comrades sheltered in their trench at Thiepval Wood waiting for the barrage to cease so they could walk across no-man's-land as instructed and capture the German trenches.

In preparation for this apparently easy task, Billy was involved in distributing the Mills grenades or bombs. Picking up a box, he cut the binding cord holding the lid, when it slipped and two grenades fell out, losing their safety pins. With the trench packed with his comrades and knowing that there was only

The Presbyterian Church in Ireland.

To express deep sympathy with those sorrowing for the loss of

your Son Wm Frederick McFadzean who *died in action sacrificing his life for others*

who gave his life in defence of his country.

Thomas West, D.D. Moderator of the General Assembly.

"Greater love hath no man than this, that a man lay down his life for his friends."

McFadzean, William, condolence scroll.

four seconds before the bombs exploded, he threw himself on the grenades. The blast was smothered by his body and he was killed instantly. Two privates were injured, including one standing nearby whose leg had to be amputated. Nonetheless, Billy McFadzean's prompt self-sacrifice saved many from death or injury.

His body was badly mutilated and, as the remains were carried away, his comrades removed their helmets as a salute. In the confusion and mayhem of the first day of the battle, McFadzean's body was never found. He was recommended for the Victoria Cross, the first of fifty-one VCs to be awarded for the Somme campaign. In 1917, a service was held at Billy's Newtownbreda Presbyterian Church, where the minister quoted from St John's Gospel: 'Greater love hath no man that this that a man lay down his life for his friends.'

McFadzean, William, VC.

68

Donald Bell – The Only Professional VC Footballer

Standing over 6ft tall and strongly built, Donald Bell was a natural athlete. When he left school, he took a junior teaching job at Westminster School and supplemented his low wage by playing for Crystal Palace FC. When he moved back north, he joined Bradford Park Avenue as a professional footballer and played at right back from 1912 to 1914. He was very quick for a back, running 100 yards in 10.5 seconds, and helped his club secure promotion to the First Division. With the outbreak of war, he asked to be released from his club contract to join the Army. He was soon commissioned into the Green Howards and was sent to the Albert section of the Somme battle.

On the fifth day, he used his speed and determination to great effect. Advancing about a mile south of Contralmaison, an enemy machine gun opened fire from the flank and inflicted casualties. Second Lieutenant Bell called to a corporal and private to follow him as he dashed down a communications trench towards the troublesome machine gun. Then, clambering out of the trench, Bell sprinted across open ground straight at the enemy position. Taken by surprise, the Germans reacted too late as Bell hurled a grenade with his left hand and fired his revolver with his right. The machine gun nest was quickly neutralised and the three men ran onto the German trench and began throwing grenades; Bell estimated that they killed and wounded at least fifty Germans. Bell's bravery enabled his battalion to go on to capture their objective.

Bell, Donald, Bradford Park Avenue.

Bell, Donald.

Bell, Donald VC Helmet.

With typical modesty, Bell wrote to his mother: 'I must confess that it was the biggest fluke alive and I did nothing. I chucked the bomb and it did the trick.' On 10 July, his luck ran out in an attack near La Boiselle. A party of Germans were spotted erecting a barricade and machine gun position, and needed to be attacked before they completed their work. Donald Bell led his bombing team across broken ground and was well ahead of his men when a bullet hit the top of his helmet. Staggering on, he threw a grenade just as a shell landed alongside, killing him.

His VC was received by his recently married wife and is now on display at the National Football Museum, Manchester. He was further honoured in 2000 when the Players Football Association erected a handsome memorial on the site of his VC action.

69

Lionel Rees – A Full and Adventurous Life

I t was not only the Army that was involved in the events of 1 July 1916 on the Somme. High above the battlefield, a desperate and one-sided fight was going on between ten German two-seaters and one single-seat Vickers F.B.5 Gunbus. Witnessed by soldiers in the anti-aircraft batteries, the unfolding action resulted in the only aerial Somme VC.

Lionel Wilmot Brabazon Rees was born in Caernarvon on 31 July 1884. Leaving the Royal Military Academy, Lionel Rees was commissioned in the Royal Artillery. During this period, he distinguished himself as an exceptional marksman. He could hit a card held by a trusting colleague with his service revolver with either hand at a range of 25 yards. He gained his Royal Aero Club certificate in January 1913, thus becoming one of the few qualified officers trained in aerial tactics. At the outbreak of the war he joined the Royal Flying Corps as a captain.

In the summer of 1915, he spotted a Fokker monoplane over the front line and joined the battle. Circling around each other, shots were exchanged. Rees' Gunbus was hit in the lower port wing, but he managed to get in a burst of fire that downed the Fokker behind enemy lines. He thus became the first designated fighter pilot to take part in an aerial combat. After several 'kills', Rees was awarded the Military Cross and

Rees, Lionel. His ketch 1st May.

Rees, Lionel.

given command of No.32 Squadron, equipped with the Airco DH.2, a new pusher-type single-seat scout machine.

On the opening morning of the Battle of the Somme, the squadron was out early accompanying a bombing raid against Don and Lille. As commander, Rees had been ordered not to cross the front line so he patrolled just behind the British trenches and waited for the bombers to return from their mission. He spotted what he thought was the returning aircraft but as they drew nearer he realised that he was flying straight into a black-crossed formation of German two-seater aircraft, mostly Rumplers and Albatroses. Despite being outnumbered ten to one, Rees continued his ascent and prepared to attack. In the unequal contest, Rees downed two German machines, damaged two others and broke up the enemy attack. Rees was seriously wounded in the leg but managed to return safely. His heroic action was rewarded with the Victoria Cross.

He remained in the newly formed RAF until he retired in 1932. Still hungering for adventure, he bought a ketch called the *May* and spent some months learning how to handle her. On 2 July 1933, he left Falmouth on his solo adventure. After thirty-three days, he reached the Azores, where he spent two weeks on repairs and replenishing his rations. Leaving the Azores, he ran into bad weather and learned of a hurricane approaching Cuba. He altered course for the Bahamas and on 21 October he dropped anchor in Nassau harbour. In the Second World War, having 'done his bit' for a rather ungrateful Royal Air Force, Rees returned to the Bahamas. In 1947, he caused quite a stir amongst the white community in Nassau when he married Sylvia Williams, the 18-year-old daughter of a black family on the island of Andros. Over the years, they had three children. Sadly, this new-found family life was cut short when Rees was diagnosed with leukaemia and forced to return to England for treatment. He came back to spend his last days in the Bahamas, where he died on 28 September 1955.

70

Thomas Jones – The VC Who Captured 102 Germans

As the Battle of the Somme ground on, an ordinary private soldier performed an extraordinary VC feat that caught the imagination of the British public. Thomas Jones was a short unassuming man who was born at 39 Princess Street, Runcorn. He worked at the Union Salt Works (later I.C.I), Runcorn and joined the Runcorn Volunteers (Earl of Chester's Rifles). He was nicknamed 'Todger', a name that stuck with him for the rest of his life. When the war started, he transferred to the Cheshire Regiment and was sent to France. On 25 September 1916 to the east of Morval, he was with his company covering the advance. One of his friends had just been shot by a German sniper, which prompted Jones to go and 'settle the score'. He spotted a sniper about 200 yards away and, without covering fire, went out into no-man's-land alone. He was shot twice; in his helmet and through his coat. Closing with the sniper, he managed to kill him. As he drew close to the enemy trench, two Germans waved a white flag but Jones, having been warned about their misuse of the flag, shot both men.

Continuing his solitary advance, he reached some dugouts, where he shot two officers. This seemed to demoralise the Germans, who thought Jones was part of a large attack. He managed to disarm them and, with the help of four comrades, captured 102 prisoners and marched them back under fire to his own lines. The whole episode had been witnessed by at least eleven officers, who did not hesitate in recommending Jones for the Victoria Cross, which was gazetted a month later. He later added to his tally when he was awarded the Distinguished Conduct Medal in 1918 for delivering messages through an intense barrage fire.

He returned home to a great reception and his feat in capturing 102 Germans was rewarded with many gifts and receptions. He lived out the rest of life in the only house he knew at 39 Princess Street, Runcorn.

Jones, T, helmet.

Jones, Thomas in Runcorn.

71

Joseph Watt and His 'David and Goliath' Action

One of the more bizarre attempts to combat the U-boat menace was to string about fifty drifter fishing boats across the 62-mile wide Straits of Otranto; the narrowest part between Italy and the island of Corfu. The thinking was to snare any U-boats trying to leave the Adriatic Sea for the Mediterranean. The drifters were backed by Italian destroyers, aircraft and kite balloons, and it was unsurprising that this strategy did little to impede the enemy submarines. Inducted into the Royal Naval Patrol Service, the former fishing vessels were painted a naval grey and armed with a single 6-pounder gun mounted at the bow.

Watt VC presentation watch.

HM Drifter *Gowanlea* was commanded by Skipper Joseph Watt RNR, a fisherman from Fraserburgh, Scotland. He and his crew of nine endured weeks of monotony holding station across the Otranto Straits. The Austrian Navy, operating out of Catarro, decided to break up this irritating barrage and sent three cruisers, including the four-funnelled *Novara*, to sink the drifters. In the early hours of 15 May 1917, the heavily armed Austrians approached to about 100 yards of the drifters and ordered the crews to abandon their vessels before sinking them. Most complied but Joseph Watt urged his crew to give 'three cheers for a fight to the finish'.

Fred Lamb, in charge of the 6-pounder, opened fire with no discernible effect on the *Novara*. The cruiser responded with a salvo that disabled the gun, detonating a box of ammunition that badly wounded Lamb. This heavy response effectively ended *Gowanlea*'s role as David to *Novara*'s Goliath. Crippled, *Gowanlea* slowly pulled away and rendered assistance to fellow drifter *Floandi*, which had suffered more casualties than Watt's vessel. Altogether, fourteen drifters were sunk and three badly damaged. Recommendations were made for Watt and Lamb to receive the Victoria Cross and another 119 men's names were put forward for recognition, including forty-five for the Conspicuous Gallantry Medal. Although Rear Admiral Mark Kerr, commanding the Adriatic squadron, was keen to recommend this rather excessive amount of awards, it was scaled down. Watt did receive the Victoria Cross, while Fred Lamb, who subsequently lost a leg during the short fight, received the Distinguished Service Medal. There were some who thought that Watt's VC did not come up to the standards required but their misgivings were overruled. He was further extravagantly decorated by the Allies, receiving the French Croix de Guerre and the Italian Silver Medal for Military Gallantry.

After the war, Joseph Watt returned to captaining his own fishing boat out of Fraserburgh, shunning all publicity and never speaking of his VC action. There may have been an element of guilt that his action was so brief and he failed to inflict any damage on the enemy. Nonetheless, his grit in taking on a large warship was recognised by the citizens of Fraserburgh and he was presented with a gold watch by George Walker, a local businessman.

Joe Watt and Fred Lamb in colour.

72

Edward Mott – The First VC of 1917

The British Army survived the pyrrhic victories of the Somme campaign, which effectively ended in November 1916. There was tacit agreement between the opposing armies that major attacks would be suspended during the bitter winter months and the soldiers settled down to reinforce their positions in preparation for the new year. The new commander, Field Marshall Douglas Haig, wished for more aggressive acts to qualify for the Victoria Cross and downgraded acts of compassion such as rescuing a comrade, or more particularly officers, as counter-productive to the overall war effort. As a consequence, men such as Sergeant Edward Mott, who would single-handedly capture an enemy machine gun position, were favourably considered for a Victoria Cross.

Edward John Mott was born on 4 July 1893 in the village of Drayton, Berkshire. In 1910, he enlisted in the Border Regiment at the age of 17 and took part in the 1915 Gallipoli Campaign. He was soon making a name for himself when

Mott, Edward VC.

he rescued his injured commanding officer and, despite being wounded, led his men in an attack for which he was awarded the DCM.

Evacuated from Gallipoli, the Border Regiment was sent to the Western Front. At the request of the French, the British extended their line 5 miles south of the River Oise. On 27 January 1917, the Border Regiment along with the Inniskilling Fusiliers mounted an attack in freezing conditions on the Landwehr Trench just south of Le Transloy. They were supported by a barrage along the 750-yard front and, as the infantry moved forward, they captured 117 prisoners. At this point, the attack was stalled by an enemy machine gun. Sergeant Mott had been wounded in the eye but took it upon himself to work his way over the frozen ground and make a flank attack.

Mott, Edward VC group held by Fitzwilliam Museum.

Mott, Edward, captured German-Machine-Gun.

The frost-hardened ground helped him in the speed with which he was able to close on the machine gunner, who was taken by surprise. In a brief struggle, Mott overpowered the German and made him prisoner. He then collected the machine gun and made his way back to his own lines. The Borderers were then able to take their objective.

Mott was recommended for the Victoria Cross, which he received on 4 April 1917 from the King at Buckingham Palace. Whether through negligence or misfortune, a fair number of VCs from the First World War had to be replaced. One such was that of Edward Mott. It would appear that his group was sold by Baldwin's before 1928 to an American collector and, on 9 August 1937, Mott claimed a replacement. The original group (ref.373) is currently held by the Fitzwilliam Museum, Cambridge, and the replacement VC, along with the captured enemy machine gun, is displayed by the Border Regiment Museum, Carlisle.

73

Albert Ball – Lone Wolf of the Skies

Britain's first celebrity fighter pilot was a 21-year-old from Nottingham named Albert Ball. He was the son of a plumber who later rose to become the Mayor of Nottingham. Albert was a determined youth with no fear of heights. He demonstrated his lack of vertigo to a steeplejack he accompanied to the top of a factory chimney; standing upright, Albert walked around the narrow edge admiring the view. After joining the local Notts and Derby (Sherwood Foresters) Regiment at the start of the war, he grew restless at the lack of action. Taking flying lessons, he transferred to the Royal Flying Corps, gaining his pilot's wings in January 1916.

Albert initially flew the slow but stable two-seat B.E.2c reconnaissance aircraft, but

Ball, Albert.

hungered for a faster single-seat fighter. His wish was granted when he joined the Nieuport Scout-equipped 11 Squadron. Unhappy with the hygiene levels of his billet, he built himself a hut next to his Nieuport's hangar and cultivated a garden. He also acted as his own aircraft mechanic, something that set him aside from his fellow pilots. Despite his lone wolf persona, he was polite and affable but seldom interested in the social life of the squadron.

He had seventeen 'kills' to his name and was promoted to captain. The first of his many gallantry awards was the Military Cross, to be followed in September by the DSO and then a Bar. Recognising within himself signs of battle fatigue, he requested home leave. Here he found that he had become a household name with the British public and was mobbed in the streets of Nottingham. Attending his investiture, Albert received his MC and double DSO from the King at Buckingham Palace. This was followed a week later by a citation in *The London Gazette* for a third Bar to his DSO; at the age of 20, he was the first man to receive three DSOs.

After his lengthy home leave, he was anxious to return to France. He was assigned to 56 Squadron, a newly formed fighter squadron, equipped with the new S.E.5, an aircraft that Ball did not like. He requested a Nieuport Scout for alternate use, which was granted, and during the next few months his tally mounted. On 7 May 1917, his last day alive, he jotted in his pocket diary: 'Gardening in morning. Patrol at night. Combat with four Albatros Scouts. Got one of them down.' Flying an S.E.5, he led an eleven-strong patrol hunting German aircraft. Within an hour,

Combats in the Air.

Squadron: **No. 11**   Date: 2. 7. 16.

Type and No. of aeroplane: Nieuport Scout A 134.   Time: 5-30 p.m.

Armament: Lewis Gun on Foster mounting.   Duty: PATROL.

Pilot: 2/Lieut. A. Ball.   Height: 10,000 ft.

Observer: ------

Locality: MERCATEL.

Remarks on Hostile machine :—Type, armament, speed, etc.

Roland Scout, 2 Seater.

Rear Gun.

Speed, about 100 m.p.h.

—— Narrative. ——

6 Rolands were seen coming towards lines from MERCATEL.

4 F.E's and Nieuport crossed lines about 10,000 ft. The Rolands split up, and were attacked by two of the four F.E's and the Nieuport. The other F.E's circled round and returned.

One of the Rolands engaged by an F.E. was seen to dive and crash near road MERCATEL- ARRAS. The Nieuport dived and shot one drum into near side of a second machine. This also dived and crashed on Road MERCATEL-ARRAS. The second F.E., attacked a third Roland, but Nieuport having turned, did not see result.

This combat was observed by Vickers 7820, which reports seeing 2 H.A's following rapidly.

A Ball

2/Lieut.
No. 11 SQUADRON,
R. F. C.

Major,
Commanding No. 11 Squadron, R. F. C.

Ball, Albert Combat report.

Above: Ball, Albert, Presentation box.

Left: Ball, Bullet through windshield.

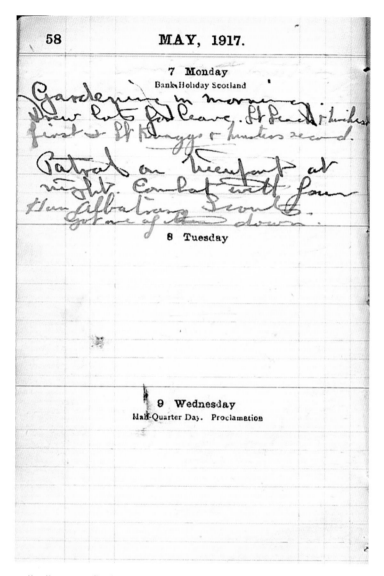

Ball, Albert VCs, final war entry diary.

they were involved in a sprawling combat across the evening sky. A fellow pilot saw Ball chase a red Albatros D.III as it disappeared into a large cloud bank. Three German officers saw the red Albatros crash near the village of Annoeullin and a few minutes later Albert Ball's S.E.5 emerged flying upside down. He descended in a shallow dive before crashing. When examined, his body and aircraft showed no signs of combat damage and it was later concluded that Ball had become disorientated in the cloud. He had somehow inverted his airplane, which killed the engine and caused the crash. The Germans gave Albert Ball a military funeral, and on 8 June 1917 it was announced that he was to be awarded the Victoria Cross. Modern research has more accurately found that Albert Ball accounted for more than sixty-seven enemy aircraft.

74

Charles Bonner – Q-Ship Hero

One of the most closely guarded secrets of the First World War was known to the Germans as a *U-Boot Falle*, or U-boat trap. To the British the innocent-looking merchantmen were known as Q-Ships, named after their home port of Queenstown in Ireland.

A lone tramp steamer appeared a soft target and was enough to lure an enemy submarine to the surface. The Q-Ship's cargo was either balsa wood or cork so they would remain afloat, encouraging the submarine to surface and sink them with their deck gun. On the surface the

Bonner on right with Gordon Campbell 1920.

No. 1.

Dated _____18 August_____ 191 7

THIS IS TO CERTIFY that Mr. _Chas. G. Bonner_____ DSC _____

has served as _____Lieutenant RNR_____ on board H.M.S. _Pargust, Dunraven_

under my command, from the __10th__ day of __~~June~~ March__ 19 17

to the _____18th_____ day of _____August_____ 191 7., during which period

he has conducted himself* _Entirely to my satisfaction. He displayed exceptional zeal and bravery in the face of the enemy, Whilst on board the ship. When the Officers were awarded a V.C by selection_

Gordon Campbell { Captain
{ H.M.S. _Dunraven_

* Here the Captain is to insert in his own handwriting the conduct of the Officer.

Bonner, Campbell's report.

U-boat was vulnerable and the Q-Ship would drop its panels to reveal her own armament and open fire.

One man who had become adept in this deadly game was Charles Bonner, better known as Gus. He was an experienced merchant seaman and was in Antwerp when the Germans invaded. Gus applied to join the Belgian Army, but this aroused suspicions that he was a spy. He crossed to England and immediately volunteered for the Royal Naval Reserve. Gus soon came to the attention of Commander Gordon Campbell, the most successful of the Q-Ship masters, and was taken on as his second officer on Q-Ship *Pargust*. On 7 June 1917, Gus was awarded the Distinguished Service Cross for his part in the sinking of *UC29*.

The *Pargust* had been badly damaged so Gus moved with Gordon Campbell to the 3,000-ton collier *Dunraven*. It was here that Gus Bonner displayed his endurance and pluck in one of the most famous Q-Ship encounters. Gus was in charge of the 4in gun hidden on the poop or aft deck; it also sat above the magazine and store of depth charges. On 7 August, U-boat *UC71* began shelling *Dunraven* and one landed among the depth charges, blowing Gus from his hiding place and landing him on the deck some yards distant. Recovering consciousness, Gus crawled back to his position just as two shells hit the poop deck, setting it on fire. Acrid black smoke enveloped the crew, several of whom were wounded. The fire threatened to ignite the magazine below but still Gus and his crew remained at their post waiting for Campbell's chance to fire at the enemy. The thick smoke from the poop drifted across the water, obscuring Campbell's view. After about

Bonner, certificate detailing his injuries.

fifteen minutes Campbell was ready to bring three of his 12-pound guns into action. *UC71* responded and hit *Dunraven's* magazine with a terrific explosion, which blew the gun crew into the air. One landed in the sea and was picked up. Incredibly, the others had their falls broken by the dummy deck cargo, although Bonner was badly injured. Burned and concussed, Gus managed to climb to the bridge and apologise to Campbell: 'I am sorry Sir to leave the gun without permission, but I believe I was blown up.'

UC71 escaped and *Dunraven* sank, despite hours of coaxing her back to port. Campbell singled out Gus Bonner for the VC and recommended him to be given command of his own ship.

75

Alfred Kinght – Extraordinary Heroism at Passchendaele

The year 1917 will always be remembered for one of the worst battles of the Great War. Other terrible battles were fought during that year but none could match the sheer misery of Passchendaele. The indelible image is of men struggling through glutinous mud, praying that they would not fall into one of the numerous water-filled shell holes to die a hideous death. Despite the dreadful conditions, a large number of men performed feats of bravery that

PO Rifles Fovant Down, badge, Wilts.

Knight, Alfred portrait.

Knight, Alfred road sign.

were rewarded with the Victoria Cross. Coming from the Ladywood district of Birmingham, Alfred Knight was employed by the Post Office. In 1914, he joined the 2/8th London Regiment (Post Office Rifles) but spent the first two years in camps in England. One included the camp on Fovant Down, Wiltshire. Here the Post Office Rifles added their cap badge emblem to other units who had cut the turf exposing the chalk beneath.

In early 1917, the regiment arrived on the Western Front and was present at the Battle of Bullecourt, where Knight saved a wounded man. In early September, the Rifles were involved in the hellish Battle of Passchendaele and, on 20 September, Sergeant Knight was a member of B Company which manoeuvred its way slowly to the enemy-held Hubner Trench. In reality this was a series of water-filled shell holes. Under cover of a British barrage, the Rifles advanced but found their way blocked by a machine gun. With their officers killed or wounded, the advance stalled. Knight grabbed the initiative. Rushing, or rather staggering, through the mud in the face of heavy fire, he bayoneted the gunners and captured the machine gun. He then went to repeat this action against another enemy nest, enabling his company to advance.

Because of the heavy casualties, Knight took command of 6 Platoon and the remnants of another. Advancing further, Alfred Knight found himself trapped in waist-deep mud and under fire. With bullets splattering the mud around him, he managed to kill six of the enemy. After he was extricated, he took part in a flanking attack that enabled the regiment to take the position. In later years he marvelled how he escaped being killed: 'All my kit was shot away … Everything went, in fact. Bullets rattled on my steel helmet – there were several significant dents and one hole … part of my book was shot away in my pocket. A photograph case and a cigarette-case probably saved my life from one bullet, which must have passed under my arm-pit – quite close enough to be uncomfortable.' For his sustained gallantry, Knight was awarded the Victoria Cross and later commissioned. He was feted in the Midlands and in 2006 a road in Ladywood, Birmingham, was named after him.

76

Frederick Greaves – The Miner Hero

Fred Greaves was born on 16 May 1890, and was the oldest of twelve children. At the age of 13 he left school to work as a coal miner at Markham Colliery near Chesterfield, Derbyshire. In his late teens, Fred nearly died when he was run over by a coal truck, breaking both his legs and crushing his pelvis. He would spend the next two years in Chesterfield Hospital recovering from his injuries. On his release from hospital, the doctor suggested that he take up cycling as part of his physiotherapy to rebuild his wasted muscles. Fred took up this advice and joined the Sheffield Cycling Club and excelled as a sportsman despite his injuries. In 1914, he was the Derbyshire champion over 50 and 100 miles. He was a teetotaller and a member of the Barlborough Primitive Methodist Church, to which he regularly sent donations while serving in the Army. In 1914, like many others, Fred volunteered for service in the Army with his brother, but because of his injuries, Fred was rejected and his brother accepted for service. Fred was finally taken into the 9th Battalion of the Sherwood Foresters on 26 February 1915 and fought in the Gallipoli campaign.

In 1916, his regiment was sent to the Western Front and on 4 October 1917, he performed his VC act at Poelcappelle, a section of the Passchendaele battle. Now a corporal, Fred Greaves' action was recalled by one of his men: 'Our force ran into one of the enemy blockhouses and we were caught between two groups of machine-gun posts. The officers and men went down with the exception of Greaves … He saw what was required. Shouting to the men not to mind, he went forward with some bombs in his hand … he seemed to be running through bullets. Greaves got around the pillbox and hurled in a couple of bombs and the fire from the pillbox ceased. He made his way inside and brought out

Greaves' Bullet.

2nd Lieut. Hy. Greaves, D.S.O., M.C., and Sergt. F. Greaves, V.C.

Greaves, Fred with Harry Greaves DSO MC.

four machine-guns in succession. That saved the day for us.'

That afternoon the German counter-attacked and, with no officers, Corporal Greaves took control. 'The enemy attacked in masses. Greaves went about among the men, encouraging them, and the outnumbered Foresters gradually recovered the ground given up ... That this result was achieved was due entirely to the brilliant leadership and courage of Greaves.' These events were not isolated for Greaves had previously performed other feats of bravery, including single-handedly capturing a machine gun post. Promoted to sergeant, Fred Greaves was awarded the Victoria Cross. When he arrived back in England, his uniform was beyond repair and so he travelled to London in his civilian clothes to collect his replacement uniform in readiness for his investiture at Buckingham Palace. A woman sat opposite Fred in the train carriage, and seeing Fred in civilian attire in a time of war, dropped a single white feather on his lap as a the symbol of her contempt for his cowardice!

After the Armistice of 1918, Fred went back to work as a miner at Barlborough. In 1938, he was awarded the Order of Jerusalem from the St John's Ambulance for his efforts in the aftermath of the Markham Pit Disaster, which claimed seventy-nine lives. For nearly thirty-six years, Fred had carried a souvenir around with him from the 1916 Beaumont Hamel Salient Front; a German bullet embedded in the back of his thigh. Almost thirty-six years after being shot, he was down the pit with his colleagues when he exclaimed, 'Ouch, that will be me bullet.' His friends thought he was joking until he had it removed at Chesterfield Hospital later that day.

77

Cecil Kinross – The Man Who Opened to Door to Victory

One of the war's more unconventional and scruffiest VC heroes was Cecil John Kinross. He was born the third of five children, at Dews Farm, Harefield, Middlesex, on 17 February 1896. In 1912, the Kinross family immigrated to Canada and settled on a prairie farm at Lougheed, Alberta, about 90 miles south-east of Edmonton. When the war broke out, the tall 22-year-old Kinross enlisted in Canadian Overseas Expeditionary Force and sailed for England at the beginning of 1916. After a short spell of training, he joined the 49th (Edmontons) Battalion and was sent to France.

Kinross suffered shrapnel wounds during the disastrous Canadian attack on Regina Trench on 9 October 1916, where the 49th took fifty per cent casualties. When he recovered, he was part of the

Kinross Mount.

great victory on Vimy Ridge. There followed an interlude with the brigade engineers before he re-joined the 49th as they entered the final stages of the dreadful Battle of Passchendaele. For three months, British and Australian troops had inched their way through acres of mud towards the German position on Passchendaele Ridge at the cost of 100,000 casualties.

On the morning of 30 October 1917, the Canadian 7th Brigade put in an attack on the north-west outskirts of what remained of Passchendaele village. The creeping artillery barrage was not effective and there were many casualties, particularly from a well-sited pillbox. By 6.30 am, the attack had stalled and men were huddling for shelter in shell holes.

After enduring the point-blank machine gun fire, Kinross decided to do something about it. Stripping off the 170lb of equipment that the attacking soldiers carried, he picked up his rifle and a bandolier and sprinted for the pillbox. Jumping into the position, he shot, bayoneted and clubbed the six Germans, and destroyed the machine gun. This single act of bravery enabled the Canadians to advance 300 yards and a week later, the long battle for Passchendaele was finally won.

Even when he received his Cross at Buckingham Palace on 6 April 1918, trouble dogged him. Appearing unsoldierly, he was

Kinross, Cecil.

arrested by two military policemen, who accused him of wearing a VC ribbon to which he was not entitled. Not until he produced the Cross and showed them his name engraved on the reverse were they convinced.

He returned to Lougheed, where the Canadian Government gave him 160 acres of land to farm. Here he remained for the rest of his life, a confirmed bachelor until his death in 1957. In 1951, he was immortalised when a 10,000ft mountain in Jasper National Park was named in his honour.

78

Stanley Boughey – Blackpool's First VC

Stanley Henry Parry Boughey had several places that claimed him as their son. He was born in Ayrshire, Scotland, on 9 April 1896 but, at a very early age, he was brought to live on a relative's farm just outside Nantwich in Cheshire. When he was 9, the family moved to Blackpool. He grew to be a keen sportsman, a devout churchgoer and a member of the Blackpool St John's Ambulance Brigade. Despite being just 17 years old, he was called up by the Red Cross and sent to France in October 1914. After helping in hospitals at Boulogne and Dunkirk, Stanley was transferred to the transport section and served with ambulances in different parts of northern France.

In April 1916, he volunteered for the Perthshire Yeomanry and applied for a commission. Completing his officer training, he was gazetted to the 4th Battalion, Royal Scots Fusiliers, and sent to Egypt. From there the regiment was sent to Palestine, from where he wrote a humorous letter to his brother beginning with: 'As you will see I have now reached the Promised Land and am kept exceedingly busy looking for the milk and honey which was supposed to flow in this part of the universe, but up to now the only flowing things in this part are plenty of nasty explosive shells sent over (all free) by a benevolent enemy.' The 4th Battalion was part of General Allenby's Egyptian Expeditionary Force that pushed the

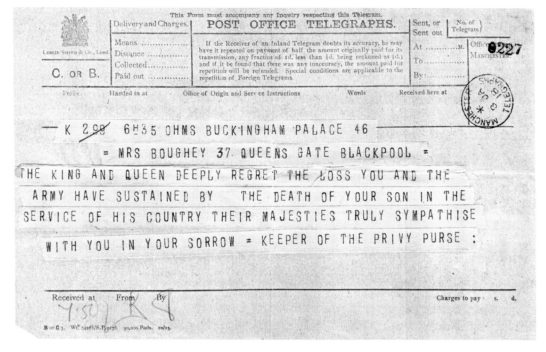

Boughey, Stanley Henry VC telegram to his mother.

Turks north through Palestine and by the end of 1917 it had established a new line south-west of Jerusalem.

On 1 December at El Burf, a Turkish assault battalion manned by German storm troopers made a sudden counter-attack that threatened the British position. It was here that Second Lieutenant Boughey performed his VC action. The Regimental War Diary records that: 'D Coy bombers were sent for and most gallantly and determinedly led by 2nd Lieut. S. Boughey, succeeded after a very hot encounter in bombing the enemy down the forward slope of the hill and eventually forcing the enemy on this part of the line to surrender. Boughey was shot in the head just as the enemy put up their first white flag.' According to his citation, Boughey, 'rushed forward alone with bombs right up to the enemy, doing great execution and causing the surrender of a party of thirty'.

Sadly, Stanley Boughey lingered for three days before dying of his wound. A brief telegram informing his mother of his death was followed by a more personal letter from his commanding officer. Blackpool made a great show of honouring its young hero with several memorials.

Boughey, Stanley VC.

79

Charles Train – The London Scottish VC

The battle for Jerusalem was approaching its end and it was the VC action of a sergeant in the London Scottish that did much to hasten the outcome. Charles Train was a Londoner born to Scottish parents and it was of little surprise when in 1909 he enlisted in the 14th Battalion, London Regiment, better known as the London Scottish. The regiment was one of the first to be sent to France, and was soon engaged in the First Battle of Ypres. Train caught diphtheria and was invalided home. Returning to France, he was wounded and sent home a second time. In 1917, he left for Salonika,

where he spent seven uncomfortable months in this fruitless campaign. In the summer the regiment returned to Egypt and joined the push against the Turkish Army.

On 8 December 1917, in bitterly cold and wet weather, the London Scottish attacked Tumulus Hill west of Jerusalem. Pinned down at close range by two machine guns behind a line of stone sangars, the men of could do little except take cover. After about forty-five minutes, Corporal Train decided he had had enough and began to crawl forward to the end of the enemy barricade. From here he was able to enfilade the

Train, C.W. Sir Alfred Butt silver passes.

Train, Charles.

enemy. The German officer in charge fired at Train. Returning fire, Train shot and wounded the officer. Firing a rifle grenade, Train disabled one of the machine gun crew. His accurate rifle fire accounted for many of the Turks, who began to retreat. One of the crew carried the other machine gun on his back and Train brought him down from 50 yards. Single-handedly, Train had cleared this obstinate barricade and captured the two effective machine guns. The following day Jerusalem fell.

Promoted to sergeant, Train was presented with his VC ribbon but it was not until 6 August 1918, at a ceremony near St Omer, that Train was invested with his VC by the King. Train was only one of twenty VC recipients presented with the Cross during five of the King's visits to France between 1914 and 1918. When he returned to London he was feted at civil receptions and twice turned down offers of a commission. As a VC recipient, one of the more unusual perks offered was an ornate silver free pass into any theatre owned by the impresario Sir Alfred Butt.

In the early 1920s, Charles Train emigrated to Canada, where he died in 1965.

80

Alan Jerrard – The First RAF VC Recipient

The new air forces in the First World War allocated the term 'ace' to those pilots who could confirm the number of kills they made. The Germans first specified eight, later increased to sixteen, to be eligible to be called an ace. The French decided on five. The British were not so sure, but initially followed the French before the institution of the Distinguished Flying Cross for those pilots who scored at least eight victories.

The first RAF VC, and the only one of the Italian campaign, was Lieutenant Alan Jerrard, whose 'kill' score reached seven enemy aircraft. The awarding of the Victoria Cross was somewhat questionable, not because he made false claims, but because his two companions exaggerated the events of a dog fight on 30 March 1918.

Alan Jerrard began his Army career with the South Staffordshires before transferring to the

Jerrard silver presentation bowl.

Royal Flying Corps. In 1917 he was flying a French-built Spad single-seat fighter and became separated from his patrol by mist and low cloud. Flying low, he hoped to find his bearings when he spotted a German convoy of transport vehicles. Diving, he raked the convoy with machine gun fire before climbing into the clouds. To his dismay, his engine died and he was forced to crash-land, sustaining serious facial injuries.

In February 1918, he was sent to join 66 Squadron in Italy. Now equipped with the Sopwith Camel, Jerrard shot down a Berg single-seat scout and destroyed an enemy observation balloon, followed by the downing of an Albatros. On 30 March, he took off with Captain Peter Carpenter and Lieutenant H.R. Eycott-Martin. The three Camels spotted four Albatros scouts escorting a two-seat Rumpler reconnaissance aircraft. Observed by his flying companions, Jerrard managed to down one of the Albatroses, before, they claimed, flying low and shooting up the enemy aerodrome at Mansue. This was packed with aircraft and they said he destroyed at least one. His colleagues said he then went on to destroy a third Albatros before being shot down by the Austrian ace Benno Fiala von Fernbrugg. Jerrard was captured and learned later that he had been awarded the VC.

Both Carpenter and Eycott-Martin, in an unsigned report, claimed they saw Jerrard attack the airfield despite being engaged with the enemy aircraft and the poor visibility. Jerrard had only hazy recollection of the day's fighting and part of his official interrogation states: 'I attacked an Albatros D fighter successfully then having lost height during the dogfight, my engine started to misfire and run rough. I was pursued by other Austrian fighters and eventually shot down.' Nowhere in the interrogation did he mention attacking Mansue aerodrome. In fact, official Austrian records reveal that there was no attack on any airfield that day. His brief citation was based on what his two companions reported and Jerrard never publicly revealed what happened.

When he returned from captivity, he was presented with his VC and a handsome silver gilt bowl by the members of the Staffordshire Territorial Force in recognition of a very gallant action.

Jerrard, Alan VC.

81

Harry Cross – And David Niven

Brought up in poverty, Norfolk-born Harry Cross married at 17 and seemed destined to work in poorly paid labouring jobs. His teenage wife had a succession of children and between 1914 and 1917 they lost two boys and two girls. He joined the 21st (Surrey) London Regiment in 1917 but soon transferred to the newly formed Machine Gun Corps (MGC), known as the 'Suicide Club'. Armed with the effective Vickers water-cooled machine guns, the crews became the first targets of the enemy. By the end of the war out of a total of 170,500 men, more than 62,000 had been killed, wounded or were missing.

After the high casualty rate of Passchendaele, the British Army suffered a shortage of men. The French were demoralised after the mutinies of 1917, while the Americans had only just started to arrive in France. The Germans, although suffering similar casualties, were now fighting on one front since the Russians had sued for peace after their revolution. It was their moment to go

Cross, Harry with David Niven.

onto the all-out attack. On 21 March 1918, the *Kaiserslacht*, or Spring Offensive, began.

Harry Cross and his 40th Battalion MGC were holding the line north of Bapaume when the rapidly advancing Germans pushed the line back, isolating his section. Although the crews managed to get away, they had to abandon two machine guns. The following morning, Cross was given permission to try and retrieve the captured guns. Armed with a service revolver, he left his trench and carefully made his way to the MGC's former position. Here he found seven Germans and the two Vickers machine guns and ammunition. Leaping from cover, he brandished the Webley revolver at the startled group, who immediately surrendered. Using sign language, Cross indicated that his prisoners should carry the captured guns and Cross' singular action was rewarded with the Victoria Cross.

In June, he added another gallantry medal to his group – the Military Medal – for holding a bridge against a German attack. He later said that it was harder earned than the VC. He experienced a further tragedy when he lost his second wife and two children during the 1941 London Blitz. In 1954 he gained nationwide fame when he responded to a plea from the actor David Niven for the loan of a genuine Victoria Cross. This

Cross, Harry.

extraordinary prop was worn in Niven's new film, *Carrington VC*. The subsequent wave of publicity brought a poignant outcome for Harry Cross. His long-lost sister, who thought he had been killed in the Blitz, made contact and they were reunited.

82

Richard Sandford – VC Hero of Zeebrugge Raid

During the last year of the Great War, the Zeebrugge Raid was the British attempt to hinder German submarine access to the North Sea via the canal from Bruges and Ostend. U-boat activity had successfully sunk many Allied vessels, merchant and naval, and a plan to seal off Zeebrugge was hatched using blockships sunk in the harbour. In order that these could enter the harbour and make their approach, a heavily armoured old cruiser, HMS *Vindictive*, would disembark some 250 Marines and sailors on the seaward side of the mile-long mole and draw the enemy's fire. Heavy bombardment from monitors and a dense smokescreen would also help to keep the enemy's attention away from the blockships.

There was one other objective that was regarded as verging on the suicidal. The heavily defended stone mole was connected to the shore by a 300-yard-long railway viaduct built on iron piers. This open latticework allowed the sea to scour out the entrance to the canal and prevent the harbour from becoming silted. It was intended to send in two obsolete submarines, each laden with five tons of amatol explosive, and detonate them beneath the viaduct, thus isolating the mole and preventing the Germans from bringing up reinforcements.

The man chosen to carry out this highly risky attack was Lieutenant Richard Sandford, who had despaired of ever seeing any action. His obsolete submarine *C3* was used to deliver the explosive charge against the railway viaduct in what was regarded as a suicide mission; only unmarried crew were considered. Although the attack was highly risky, it was not a *kamikaze* sacrifice. The crews had to be given a chance to escape and each submarine carried two motorised skiffs either side of the conning tower. As the attack got under way, one of the submarines suffered an accident, leaving Sandford to carry on alone.

Undetected in the early hours of 23 April 1918, Sandford managed to steer his time-bomb

Sandford RN VC.

HMS *Vindictive* War Memorial.

under the viaduct between two vertical piles and ran the submarine up the horizontal girder. This was the exact position he had hoped for and, hurrying below, he lit the three fuses. Clambering back on deck, he joined the crew in the skiff. The engine was started, but the current pushed them back against the submarine and the skiff's propeller snagged against the exhaust pipe and killed the engine. Five precious minutes had elapsed and still they had not moved away from amatol-laden vessel. By now the Germans had woken up and started firing at the skiff, and water started to pour in through the bullet holes. Several of the crew were wounded, including Sandford. The crew had rowed only 300 yards away, still well within the danger area, when *C3* erupted with a tremendous explosion, throwing a pillar of flame high in the sky. The blast threw the debris 800 yards and a 100-yard gap had been blown in the viaduct. It was a miracle that the great lumps of metal crashed into the sea all around the tiny boat but its crew emerged unscathed. For this act of daring Richard Sandford received the Victoria Cross but sadly died soon after during the Spanish Flu epidemic. A memorial was erected at Zeebrugge using the bow of HMS *Vindictive*.

83

Edward Mannock – The One-Eyed ACE

The RFC/RAF did not subscribe to the term 'ace' and, although men such as William Robinson and Albert Ball were internationally acknowledged for their prowess, generally the public was not aware of many of their flying VC heroes. One such was Major Edward (Mick) Mannock, who was officially recognised as Britain's highest-scoring pilot. Brought up in a military environment – his father was a corporal in the Royal Scots Grays – Mannock was a delicate child who suffered from a severe astigmatism in his left eye. He was born in the cavalry barracks at Brighton on 24 May 1887. His father deserted the family when Mick was just 13 and the youngster had to leave school to work at menial jobs to help support his mother and four siblings. He later joined his brother working as a telephone engineer and moved to Wellingborough, Northamptonshire. In early 1914, the telephone company sent him to Turkey as a field supervisor. When Turkey sided with Germany, Mannock was interned and suffered from the primitive prison conditions. Eventually he was released as 'Unfit for military duties'.

Within a year, Mick Mannock had recovered his health and joined the RFC, proving to be an outstanding pilot. In 1917, he was awarded the Military Cross and promoted to captain. Six months later he added a bar to his MC.

EXTRA PALE
* BREWED WITH *
BRITISH 'FLYER' HOPS

Flyer

3.9% ABV

BREWED to COMMEMORATE

MAJOR MICK MANNOCK VC

WELLINGBOROUGH'S OWN FLYING ACE!

FRANCE 1914-1918

*

HART FAMILY BREWERS

Mannock, Mick beer flyer.

Mannock, Mick in SE5 of 74 Sq 1918.

In March 1918, he joined No 74 Squadron equipped with S.E.5a single-seat scouts and by May was awarded the DSO followed by two more bars. His personal 'kill' rate had risen to fifty-two by the end of May. Despite his fighting prowess, Mick Mannock was not a lone wolf in the manner of Albert Ball. He briefed his men on his methods and encouraged them to act as a team rather than individuals. To his men he was the ideal flight commander.

Between 17 June and 22 July, Major Mannock accounted for eight enemy aircraft. On 26 July he shot down a DFW CV reconnaissance machine and, unaccountably in violation of his strict ruling on flying low over enemy, he swooped to deck level over trenches occupied by the Germans. He was met by a barrage of rifles and machine guns. This started a fire in the engine that spread along the side of his aircraft. Mannock crashed in a ball of flame behind enemy lines and, although the Germans buried him, the whereabouts of his remains has never been found.

At the end of the war the final VCs were awarded but Mannock's colleagues were dismayed that their leader had not been recognised. The newly appointed Air Minister, Winston Churchill, added his weight and Britain's most highly decorated and successful pilot was gazetted on 18 July 1919.

84

Cecil Sewell – Early Tank VC

One of the earliest Tank Corps VCs was awarded to Lieutenant Cecil Sewell for his outstanding bravery outside his armoured vehicle. Born in London on 27 January 1895, he was commissioned in the Royal West Kent Regiment in 1916. It was seeing the first tanks in action on the Somme that prompted him to transfer to the Heavy Section Machine Gun Corps, soon to be renamed the Tank Corps. Equipped with the notoriously unreliable rhomboid-shaped Mark IV, Sewell's only action was at Cambrai in 1917, when his tank received a direct hit from an artillery shell and burst into flame. The following year his 3rd (Light) Tank Battalion was equipped with the new Whippet tank, which in appearance resembled all succeeding designs, with a turret on top, albeit fixed and sited to the rear. Entry was through a large door at the back of the turret. Armament was four Hotchkiss .303 machine guns sited on each side of the turret and operated by one gunner. It had a top speed of 6mph, twice that of the Mark IV.

On 29 August 1918, Sewell was in command of four Whippets as they cleared the way in front of the infantry east of Bapaume. As they manoeuvred to avoid the heavy enemy fire, the tank commanded by Lieutenant Rees-Williams side-slipped into a deep shell hole, overturned and caught fire. Cecil's commanding officer wrote: 'Lieut. Sewell in the leading Whippet (about 70 yards in advance), on seeing the plight of Lieut. Rees-Williams's Car, immediately got out of his own Whippet and came to the rescue. Unaided, with a shovel, he dug an entrance to the door of the cab which was firmly jammed and embedded in the side of the shell hole; forced the door open and liberated the crew … the imprisoned crew might have burnt to death, as they were helpless to extricate themselves without outside assistance. During the whole of this time the Whippets were being very heavily shelled and the ground swept by machine gun fire at close range. On endeavouring to return to his own Car, Lieut. Sewell was unfortunately hit several times, his body being subsequently found lying beside that of his Driver/Gunner W. Knox, also killed, just outside their Tank, which at that time was within short range of several machine gun and infantry pits.'

Cecil Sewell received a posthumous VC and, most unusually, his tank was saved and put on display at the Bovington Tank Museum.

Sewell, Cecil VC Colour.

Whippet Tank.

85

Henry Tandey – Did He Spare Adolf Hitler?

There are several brave soldiers who could lay claim to be the most highly decorated Other Rank in the Great War but without doubt the winner would be Henry Tandey. In a short spell of five weeks, between 25 August and 28 September 1918, he won the Distinguished Conduct Medal and the Military Medal, culminating in the bestowal of the Victoria Cross. Outstanding though these decorations are, Henry Tandey will be forever remembered as the soldier who spared the life of Adolf Hitler. Or did he? Despite numerous articles and a thoroughly researched biography it seems as if the story comes under the heading of an 'urban legend'. There are, however, enough pointers to indicate that there are some aspects of the story that are factual.

Tandey was awarded his VC for gallantry at Marcoing by the Canal de St Quentine; a location where Adolf Hitler was absent. The 1923 painting by Fortunino Matania erroneously indicates that it is at Marcoing in 1918. In fact, the location is the first aid station at Kruiseeke Crossroads during the 1914 First Battle of Ypres and purports to show Tandy carrying a wounded man. In 1937, Hitler was made aware of Matiana's painting by Dr Otto Schewend, a member of his staff who had treated a wounded Lieutenant-Colonel Earle during the Ypres battle. After the war, Schewend obtained a copy of the painting from Earle, which Hitler displayed on his wall at Berchtesgarten. Hitler claimed that the man carrying the wounded soldier was the same man who had lowered his

Tandey, Henry.

rifle and let him pass during the 1914 Ypres battle. Hitler acknowledged the gift from the Green Howards Regiment with 'his best thanks for your friendly gift which is so rich in memories'. So far, so plausible.

The story has been further embroidered with the 1938 visit to Germany by Prime Minister Neville Chamberlain, who was shown Matiana's picture at the Berghof. Hitler asked Chamberlain to convey his greetings and gratitude to Henry

Tandey, which he supposedly did via the telephone. As Tandey did not have a telephone and there is no reference of Chamberlain ever making contact, the story has the appearance of make believe. Tandey later claimed that he had lowered his rifle to let several Germans pass as he could not shoot at a wounded enemy.

Tandey was badly wounded during his final action and immediately evacuated to England. When he recovered he was presented with his Victoria Cross in December 1919. He was further honoured with the Freedom of Leamington, which is displayed in a silver casket at the town hall.

Left: Tandey, Henry, Freedom casket Leamington.

Below: Tandy, The 1923 painting by Fortunino Matania.

Wilfred Wood – The Piave Front VC

One of the last VCs during the final throws of the Great War was awarded for the defeat of the Austrian Army on the Piave River, Italy. Wilfred Wood had left school to work at the Edgeley sheds of the London and North Western Railway (LNWR) before joining the 10th Battalion, Northumberland Fusiliers. In 1917, the regiment was sent to prop up the Italian Army, which had suffered a series of defeats after the Battle of Caporetto. On 28 October 1918, Private Wood, in charge of a Lewis machine gun, took the initiative when his company was held up by an enemy machine gun. Working his way forward, he enfiladed the enemy strong point, killed the machine gun crew and caused 140 of the enemy to surrender. Moving on, another hidden machine gun halted the advance. This time Wood charged, firing his Lewis gun from the hip and wiping out the machine gun crew. He found himself at the side of the enemy trench with a clear view along its length and was able to call on the 160 demoralised Austrians to surrender. With the Allies on the enemy's side of the river, the hundreds of prisoners surrendered and much equipment was captured, which soon heralded the end to hostilities.

On 19 December 1918, Wilf Wood received the Victoria Cross from the King at Buckingham Palace. Demobilised, Wood returned to the LNWR and trained as a fireman. Later he became a driver and worked the routes from Blackpool to Birmingham and Leeds to Liverpool. He was one of three VCs honoured when a locomotive of the 'Patriot Class' was named after him; the other two were LNWR employees J.A. Christie and E. Sykes. Wilf Woods retired from LNWR after forty-six years and died on 3 January 1982.

Wood, Wilf, Engine driver.

Wood, Wilfred VC.

William Coltman – The Most Gallantry Awards to An NCO

The highest number of gallantry awards to an NCO in the First World War was to a man who never carried a rifle. William (Bill) Coltman came from rural Staffordshire and lived in a tied cottage belonging to Lord Burton of brewery fame. Leaving school at 14, Bill worked as a gardener and was a devout member of the Plymouth Bretheren, a non-conformist Christian movement. In January 1915, Bill enlisted in the 6th Battalion, North Staffordshire Regiment.

The Bretheren had no central governing body to dictate how each man would approach the war. Bill went through basic training but decided that it was wrong for him to kill another human and volunteered as a stretcher bearer with the regiment. Bill's upbringing in the countryside gave him a good eye for the land and he soon went out alone in no-man's-land to collect the wounded. Despite his modest height, he had strength in his upper body that enabled him to bring in wounded men on his back despite the proximity of the Germans.

The first few minutes after a soldier was wounded were the most critical with regards to survival and were referred to as 'the golden hour'. Bill Coltman's first act was early on in the Battle of the Somme. Taking shelter in shell hole with the infantry, including a badly wounded sergeant, Bill decided he had to get the man back to his own lines. Lifting him on to his shoulders, he crawled back through the fire to the British lines. He went out again under heavy fire and brought in men who otherwise may have died a lingering death alone in no-man's-land. For this he received the first of several Mentioned in Despatches.

Coltman, William, with three gallantry medals.

Coltman, William VC, Stretcher bearer Brassard.

Promoted to lance-corporal, Bill was awarded his first Military Medal for rescuing an officer who had been shot and became entangled in barbed wire. He soon received a bar to his Military Medal for rescuing men who were trapped in a railway tunnel. In 1917, he received the Distinguished Conduct Medal for a sustained period of days while he roamed the battlefield searching for wounded men. He was also in action when a long-range shell landed in a village in which his regiment was resting. A nearby house was hit and collapsed. Bill and other stretcher bearers managed to pull out a young girl and her mother. The little boy could not be found but Bill stayed and searched the rubble until he located him barely alive.

On 28 September 1918, Bill Coltman was awarded a bar to his DCM for saving lives and bringing back valuable information about the advance. The following day, he went out and treated wounded Germans who had been left behind. During the operations on 3 and 4 October at Mannequin Hill, Coltman heard that British wounded were lying under fire from German machine guns and he went out alone despite the heavy fire. He found the casualties, dressed their wounds and made three dangerous return journeys to bring them back safely. For this he was awarded the highest accolade, the Victoria Cross. During three years of the war, he had exposed himself to more danger than most and had never fired a shot in anger!

88

Augustus Agar – The 'Secret VC'

The Armistice of November 1918 ended four years of slaughter that left the participants exhausted and its populations weary of war. While servicemen returned home, the politicians were left to tidy up the mess that had been left. One such mess was the unresolved problem of Russia and the Bolshevik counter-revolution that was threatening to engulf the Baltic States. Augustus (Gus) Agar was a lieutenant in the Royal Navy who had participated in an unremarkable war but belatedly was appointed to train for a new high-speed craft known as the Coastal Motor Boat (CMB). In 1919, he was summoned to the Naval Intelligence Division, where he met Sir Mansfield Cumming; 'C' of MI6. Agar was asked to undertake an operation for the Secret Service involving two CMBs, which would land and collect couriers from the coast near Petrograd. This involved passing the Russian Baltic Fleet island base at Kronstadt with its string of forts guarding the approaches to Petrograd. Picking five unmarried men, Agar found a disused yacht harbour near the Finnish–Russian border. From there, they ferried couriers in and out of Petrograd.

Agar noticed that across the Gulf of Finland two Russian battleships from

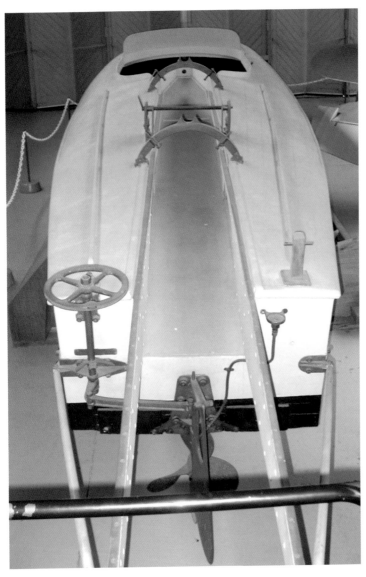

Agar, A. CMB4-Duxford.

Agar, Augustus VC.

engine problems, so Agar set off alone in the early morning hours of 17 June. He found that the two battleships had returned to Kronstadt to be replaced by a heavy cruiser, the *Oleg*, which lay at anchor. Agar wrote of the night's events: 'Throwing all caution to the winds, I put on full speed and headed straight for the *Oleg*, which was now clearly visible, and in a few minutes we were nearly on top of her. I fired my torpedo less than five hundred yards away, just as the first shot from her guns was fired at us in return. Then I quickly put the helm over, turning a complete circle. And with the sea now following us, headed westward towards the same direction from which we had approached. We looked back to see if our torpedo had hit, and saw a large flash abreast of the cruiser's foremost funnel. This was followed almost immediately by a huge column of black smoke reaching up to the top of her mast. The torpedo had found its mark.'

On 9 October 1919, entering the King's private study, Gus was invited to sit and relate the whole story. At length, the King presented Agar with his Victoria Cross. He also presented him with the DSO for his part in the subsequent Kronstadt Raid. It was to be decades later that the full story of this clandestine operation became public knowledge.

Kronstadt were bombarding the White Russian fortress of Krasnaya Gorka in Estonia. Obtaining permission from the local admiral, he loaded torpedoes on the two CMBs and set out to sink the battleships. One of the CMBs developed

89

Bernard Warburton-Lee – Hero of Narvik

Narvik, in northern Norway, was of great importance to Nazi Germany in the Second World War for she imported large quantities of Swedish iron ore from the port. The route was especially important during the winter months when the northern part of the Baltic Sea was frozen over. Narvik was only about 15 miles from the Swedish border and linked to the iron ore region by rail. Hitler's main goal was to secure Narvik and prevent Norway collaborating with the Allies. In turn, the British wanted to secure Norway to prevent

Germany using the deep water ports to attack Allied shipping in the North Atlantic. To this end, the Royal Navy dispatched a flotilla of destroyers under the command of Captain Bernard Warburton-Lee to secure Ofotfjord, leading to the port of Narvik. Unbeknown to the Admiralty, Germany had sent her own *Gruppe 1* flotilla of ten destroyers to capture Narvik.

Entering the 50-mile-long Ofotfjord, Warburton-Lee decided that the Germans were ignorant of the British presence and planned to attack the ships inside Narvik harbour. At 04.30,

Warburton-Lee wreck of Georg Thiele.

under the cover of darkness and snow squalls, HMS *Hardy*, *Hotspur*, *Havoc* and *Hunter* began their attack. Taking turns to enter the harbour entrance, the British sank two destroyers, disabled one more, and sank six supply ships, all without suffering any damage.

One of the torpedoes hit the flagship *Wilhelm Heidkamp*, causing the magazine to explode and crucially killing the *Gruppe 1* commander. After three attacks, which left the British destroyers untouched, they ran into five German warships that had been at anchor in separate fjords. The German gunnery was most accurate and quickly found its range. The *Hardy* was the first ship to be hit and her bridge was destroyed, with a mortally wounded Warburton-Lee among the casualties. With the *Hardy* taken out of action, one of her surviving officers managed to beach her and her crew were able to scramble ashore. Warburton-Lee was found to be dead and his body was later laid to rest in the nearby cemetery at Ballangen.

Local Norwegians gave refuge to the 140 surviving crew, who were later picked up by a British ship and returned to home. Captain Warburton-Lee was posthumously awarded the first Victoria Cross of the war on 2 July 1940.

Warburton-Lee, B, in dress uniform.

The remaining German destroyers found they were low on fuel and effectively bottled up in Ofotfjord. A later raid sank and beached the rest of the German flotilla and contributed to Hitler's reluctance to invade Britain until his naval losses could be replaced.

HMS Hardy flag at Narvik.

90

James Nicolson – Fighter Command's Only VC

Only one fighter pilot in the Second World War was awarded the Victoria Cross and that was during the summer of 1940 when the Battle of Britain was fought over southern skies. The pilot was 23-year-old Flight Lieutenant James Nicolson of the Hurricane-equipped 249 Squadron based at Boscombe Down. He had been in the RAF for three years but had never experienced combat before. On 16 August 1940, while patrolling to the west of Southampton, he was fired upon by a Messerschmitt 110, which wounded him and set his plane alight. Taking evasive action, he was about to bail out when he saw the enemy aircraft shoot past him. Deciding to chase after his foe, he got within range and pressed the gun button. Both aircraft were in a steep 400mph dive and Nicolson kept firing despite the flames that

Nicolson, J, helmet.

were filling his cockpit. He saw the skin of his left hand peeling off and his vision was impaired by blood pouring from a wound over his eye but he kept following the enemy aircraft until the flames forced him to bail out.

With his uniform still smouldering and his wounds starting to cause him distress, he floated down and managed to manoeuvre the chute away from the sea. Just when he was only 50ft from landing, an over-zealous Local Defence Volunteer (LDV) loosed off both barrels of his shotgun, adding to Nicolson's discomfort. Although Nicolson made light of his injuries, they were enough to hospitalise him for six months.

The wing commander of 249 Squadron recommended James Nicolson for the Distinguished Flying Cross but when it reached King George VI, he expressed surprise that the recent exploits of the Royal Air Force had not produced a single recommendation for the Victoria Cross. This comment was conveyed to Air Vice-Marshals Keith Park and Hugh Dowding, who, on 28 October 1940, changed the award to that of the Victoria Cross. Nicolson was informed of the award in early November just days before his wife gave birth to their son. Having downed just one enemy aircraft, Nicolson was heard to say: 'Now I will have to go and earn it.'

Ten days later he took his wife, mother and two sisters to Buckingham Palace for a private investiture with the King, who handed over the VC without the formal pinning on. There was

some resentment that Nicolson was the only fighter pilot to receive the Cross when others, including the celebrated and much decorated Robert Stanford Tuck, Douglas Bader and Johnnie Johnson, did not.

Promoted to wing commander, James Nicolson never again engaged in aerial combat. Commanding a Mosquito squadron in India, he lost his life on 2 May 1945 over the Bay of Bengal flying as an 'observer' on a bombing mission to Rangoon.

Nicolson, James.

91

John Beeley – VC of the Battle of Sidi Rezegh

Commencing on 17 November 1941, Operation *Crusader* was mounted to disrupt and destroy the Axis forces before they could begin their anticipated invasion of Egypt. It was a vast sprawling battle covering an area roughly the size of East Anglia and fought in the bitter conditions of mid-winter. A crucial part of the battle, which produced three VCs, was on the descending escarpments at Sidi Rezegh. On the middle escarpment was an enemy airfield, which was taken. To the north was the Sidi Rezegh Ridge occupied by the Axis defenders and in order to continue the advance this had to be taken. Three companies of The King's Royal Rifle Corps (KRRC) and a company of The Rifle Brigade totalling 400 picked their way through the wreckage on the airfield. They had to cross 2,000 yards of flat stony ground without cover and capture a 2-mile stretch of the ridge to allow the armour to get through.

Soon the German and Italian defenders opened up with machine guns and mortars, and the riflemen took heavy casualties. After three and a half hours, supported by artillery and helped by smoke and dust, the soldiers managed to get within 100 yards of the ridge. It was at this point that the first VC exploit took place.

Beeley, John grave at Sidi Rezegh.

Rifleman John Beeley was the Bren gunner of his platoon. Based in Winchester, he had enlisted in the KRRC in 1938. He had also married a local girl, Betty Davy, who was serving in the ATS. Beeley had gone into battle preoccupied with bad news from home, which may have prompted his extraordinary action. Pinned down by a strong point that contained an anti-tank gun and two machine guns, any advance seemed suicidal. Suddenly, Rifleman Beeley leapt to his feet and ran straight at the strong point, firing bursts from the hip. Clambering amongst the rocks, he was hit but it did not stop him. Pausing 20 yards from the nest, he coolly aimed and opened fire, killing or wounding the entire crew of the anti-tank gun. He was almost immediately killed by fire from other positions.

His remarkable action spurred his comrades into charging forward, carrying the ridge and capturing about 800 prisoners. John Beeley's single-handed action had enabled this important feature to be captured and was recognised with the posthumous awarding of the Victoria Cross.

Beeley, John Memorial program.

William Savage – ST Nazaire VC

escribed as 'the Greatest Raid of All', the destruction of the Normandie Dock at St Nazaire on 28 March 1942 denied the dry-dock facilities on the Atlantic seaboard to the mighty battleship *Tirpitz*. Code-named Operation *Chariot*, the audacious raid remains unique in military annals. Central to the operation was the obsolete destroyer HMS *Campbeltown*. Loaded with nearly 5 tons of explosives set to detonate by delayed fuses, she would ram the dock at full speed. Raiding parties would pour ashore and damage as much of the dock facilities as possible before making their escape. It was essential that *Campbeltown* should reach her target and she was given a protective screen of sixteen motor launches (MLs) each carrying fifteen Commandos, one motor torpedo boat (MTB) and the headquarters gunboat, *MTB314*. She would carry the raid commander, Robert Ryder, and Lieutenant-Colonel Charles Newman, leader of the Commandos. Also on board was Able Seaman William (Bill) Savage, who was the 'layer' on the forward pom-pom (the QF 1-pounder 37mm auto-cannon).

In 1939, Bill Savage joined the Royal Navy and was assigned to MTBs, taking part in

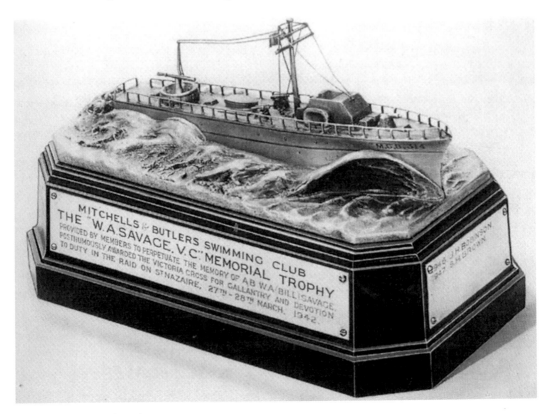

Savage, Bill memorial trophy.

Savage, William.

several clandestine missions dropping agents and Commandoes on the French coast. With such experience from these operations in enemy waters, *MTB314* was chosen to take part in Operation *Chariot*.

As the raiders left Falmouth, the crews learned of their destination on the second day. Approaching the French coast in a wide arc to fool any enemy reconnaissance, they finally entered the River Loire estuary in darkness and sailed the 6 miles to St Nazaire. With *MTB314* in the lead, followed by *Campbeltown* and two lines of motor launches, the flotilla was challenged but managed to delay their responses until they were within a mile of their target. Their German flags were lowered and the White Ensign hoisted. This was a signal for the German defences to open up from both sides of the river. Encountering a *Sperrbrecher*, a heavily armed guard ship, Bill Savage and his comrades raked her from end to end and knocked out all the crews, including that of the 88mm. Savage then fired on the pillbox on the end of the Old Mole and silenced the crew. Described as entering an archway of coloured lights, tracer bullets and shells rained down on the British ships. *MTB314* moored alongside the Old Entrance for fifteen minutes while Newman disembarked and Ryder tried to find out what was going on with the *Campbeltown*. In fact, the old destroyer had a free run at the mighty caisson with a speed that forced her bows on the top of the lock gates. By this time the whole of the basin had become a scene of chaos and carnage. The two twin 0.5in guns on *MTB314* had been put out of action and Savage's was the only one left firing. Once again he silenced the re-manned pillbox. As Ryder ordered a withdrawal, Savage was killed and his body added to the many dead littering the deck of *MTB314*.

Bill Savage was awarded a posthumous VC, which was received by his wife on 23 June 1942 at Buckingham Palace.

93

Charles Newman – The Raid's Commando Leader

The commanding officer of the Commandos who were landed at the St Nazaire docks just did not fit the description of what one would have pictured as a hard-as-nails rugged leader. Augustus Charles Newman was an avuncular, pipe-smoking businessman who played golf and entertained his men by playing jazz on the piano. He was a territorial officer in the 4th Battalion, Essex Regiment, who always took his golf clubs to Army camp. He was also a first-class organiser and when the opportunity arose, joined the Commandos. After taking part in the ill-judged Norwegian campaign,

Newman, A.C.

he was put in charge of No.1 Commando and in early 1942 he was summoned to the War Office. Here he learned that his group were to be landed and wreak destruction on the docks at St Nazaire.

The sixteen motor launches, each carrying about fifteen Commandos, were not ideal troop-carrying boats. With the naval crew, they were very crowded and the installation of an extra 500 gallon fuel tank on the upper deck increased their vulnerability. The motor gun boat *MTB314* acted as the HQ boat and this dropped Colonel Newman at St Nazaire's Old Mole. With so many motor launches sunk before they could land the Commandos, Newman had to change his strategy. He had selected a building near Bridge G at the far end of the Old Entrance to be his headquarters and led his HQ group towards it. As he walked around a corner, he 'bumped helmets' with a German and instinctively said: 'Sorry'. The German hurriedly surrendered. Newman ordered the German to go in and bring out his comrades with their hands up. Before this could be done, the HQ party were spotted and fired upon. About 113 Commandos had been landed, of which forty were only armed with pistols. They had little difficulty in dealing with the superior numbers of enemy troops, but were almost helpless under the concentrated fire from the fixed gun positions and the ships in the harbour, some of whom were firing at close quarters. Despite the withering fire, there were

Newman, Charles, Colt.455.

some telling fights with the German troops who started pouring into the area known as the Old Town inland from the Old Mole.

Newman's calm and jovial manner had the effect of reassuring everyone. With the area now effectively sealed by this unwelcome increase of enemy forces, the Commandos split into smaller parties and began what was later termed the 'St Nazaire Obstacle Race'. In order to keep clear of the streets, the Commandos clambered over back walls, through chicken coops and even through houses in an effort to evade capture and try and make for the Spanish border. Finally, Newman's group surrendered but were heartened when they heard the delayed explosion, which destroyed the Normandie dry dock. When he was liberated, Charles Newman received a well-deserved Victoria Cross.

94

Adam Wakenshaw – His Self-Sacrifice Saved Others

Brought up in abject poverty in industrial Gateshead, Adam Wakenshaw was one of six children to survive (seven died in infancy). When he was 18, he married Dorothy Ann Douglass and soon had three children. He also realised his ambition to join the Army by volunteering for the 9th (Territorial) Durham Light Infantry. When the Second World War broke out, many of the Territorial battalions were sent to France with the British Expeditionary Force. The Durhams saw action in the retreat from Belgium, during which Wakenshaw was wounded. The brigade fell back to Dunkirk, from where they were evacuated.

In February 1941, a tragedy hit the Wakenshaw family when their 7-year-old son John was killed in a road accident near his home. Adam was given compassionate leave and it was to be the last time his family saw him. The 9th Battalion was ordered to North Africa as part of The 50th (Northumbrian) Division.

The retreat from Gazala halted at Marsa Matruh, where the 8th Army attempted to fight a rearguard action, while further behind them a defensive position was being formed at

Wakenshaw's wrecked gun and grave.

El Alamein. The 151st Durham Brigade had been positioned on a flat and rocky plateau called Point 174, where it was impossible to dig in. Instead the troops sheltered behind boulders and rock-built sangers while they waited for the enemy. Totally exposed in front of the infantry were the nine 2-pounder anti-tank guns, of which Adam Wakenshaw was a crew member. About 0515 hours on 27 June 1941, the German 90th Light Division approached supported by tanks and artillery. A tracked vehicle towing a light gun came within range of Wakenshaw's gun. The 2-pounder opened fire and scored a direct hit on the engine, which stopped dead. Another German mobile gun opened fire and killed or badly wounded the crews of the little anti-tank guns. With the guns silenced, heavy mortars and artillery opened fire as the Germans moved towards the damaged tracked vehicle and the light artillery piece. If the Germans reached it they would only be 200 yards from the battalion. This was spotted by a cruelly wounded Wakenshaw, whose left arm had been blown off.

With the help of a wounded gun-layer, he managed to load five shells with one arm. A direct hit and the tracked vehicle burst into flames, with the gun damaged. Then a German round exploded close by, killing the gun-layer and further wounding Wakenshaw.

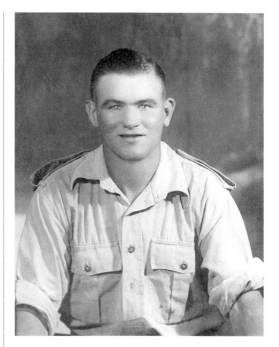

Wakenshw, Adam VC.

Painfully he dragged himself back to his gun and loaded another round, but before he could fire, a German round hit his gun, exploded the ammunition and killed him. With no anti-tank guns, the position was soon overrun. After the Germans had withdrawn, members of the 8th Battalion searched the defensive area and found Wakenshaw slumped over the breechblock. He was buried beside his gun and his young wife received his posthumous VC from the King.

95

Frank Blaker – Chindit VC

The son of a Rangoon-based Indian Army medical doctor, Frank Blaker had grown up in Burma and understood the country and its culture, giving him a rare perspective. He boarded at Taunton School and when the war started, he joined the Somerset Light Infantry. He was commissioned in 1941 and the next year joined the 9th Gurkha Rifles in India. His regiment formed part of the 4th Indian Infantry Brigade in its abortive first incursion into the Arakan. To his fellow officers

Blaker was known as 'Jim', an allusion to the cereal advertising character 'Sunny Jim', because of his cheerful nature.

Blaker and his platoon had one of the few successes when he was sent to investigate enemy activity at a village about 5 miles from Taung Bazaar. A sharp exchange of fire pushed the Japanese back to take a defensive position on a nearby ridge. Disregarding the fire from two machine guns, Blaker led his twenty-six men up the slope and forced the enemy to

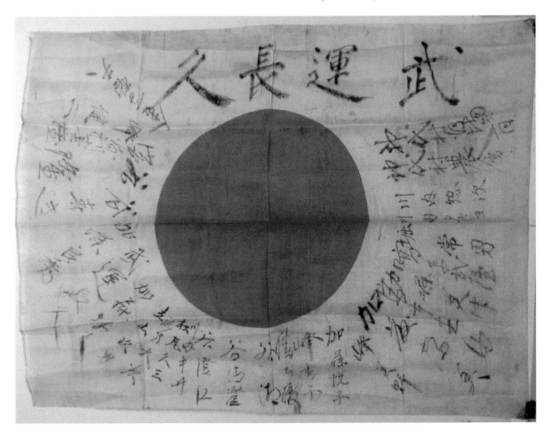

Blaker, captured Japanese Flag 2.

retreat to the south. Following up, the enemy were chased for a further 2 miles during, which the Gurkhas killed sixteen men and captured three wounded. He also captured a Japanese flag and one of the wounded officers, who carried valuable intelligence. Blaker was recommended for an immediate award of a Military Cross.

His Gurkhas were part of the first Chindit incursion behind Japanese lines and the following year were involved in the push north to take the all-important town of Myitkyina. On 9 July 1944, they came under fire from three machine guns on the steep jungle-covered sides of a ridge and Blaker went ahead of his men through heavy fire. A hand grenade burst within 2 yards and he was severely wounded in the arm. He got up and calmly moved towards the machine gun. A long burst fatally wounded him but his men rushed forward and took the ridge. Incredibly, Blaker lifted himself up and walked back 500 yards down the track before collapsing. He lingered for a few more hours and his last words to his havildar major were: 'Thank C Company for all they've done for me.

Blaker, Frank and his Medals.

Tell them I have gone from them but they must go on fighting to the end.' His was gazetted on 26 September 1944 and his VC sent to his parents.

96

Donald Cameron and Godfrey Place – The Tirpitz Raid

One of the most audacious raids in the Second World War was the submarine attack on the 43,000ton German battleship *Tirpitz*. It was doubly daring as the new X-craft miniature submarine had not been used other than in training. Their first deployment was Operation *Source*, an attempt to neutralise the heavy German warships based in northern Norway that threatened the convoys bound for Russia. Six craft were used but only two successfully carried out their attack. These two were *X6* and *X7*, commanded respectively by Lieutenants Donald Cameron and Godfrey Place.

Towed by submarines to the mouth of Sørøy Sund within the Arctic Circle, they had to travel 15 miles at night to Altafjord. With no radio contact between the miniature submarines, there was no way of knowing their whereabouts, but on 22 September 1943, *X6* and *X5* managed to penetrate the anti-submarine defences that covered the small inlet of Kafjord where the *Tirpitz* lay at anchor. Acting independently, Cameron's craft had luck when he was able to

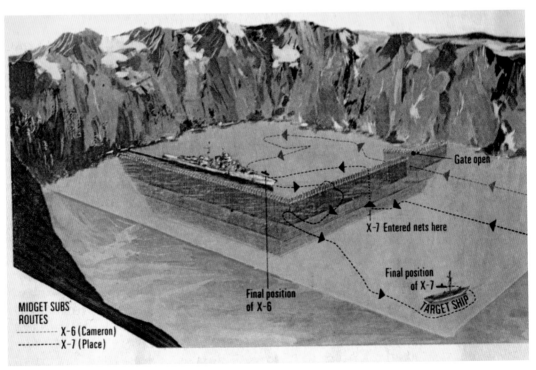

MIDGET SUBS'
ROUTES
---------- X-6 (Cameron)
---------- X-7 (Place)

Gate open

X-7 Entered nets here

Final position
of X-7

TARGET SHIP

Final position
of X-6

Cameron & Place attack on Tirpitz.

follow a trawler though a boat-gate in the anti-torpedo nets surrounding the battleship. Both craft experienced difficulties as the snow-fed layers of fresh water made it difficult to keep the crafts in trim, as one minute they passed through a patch of salt water and the next fresh.

X6 hit a rock, which drove her to the surface. In the seconds they had to submerge, Cameron saw they were just 200 yards from *Tirpitz*. With his compass smashed, he was forced to take another look though the periscope and was spotted. The alarm was raised by the lookouts. *X6* submerged and Cameron released his side tanks of amatol explosive before surfacing and surrendering. Scuttling their craft, the crew were taken on board. Meanwhile, *X7* had penetrated the torpedo net and successfully laid its charges under the bow of the battleship. In an effort to escape, *X7* became entangled in the torpedo nets and Place's crew were forced to surrender. Both crews now waited in anticipation on board the *Tirpitz* for the timed charges to explode. At 08.15 they detonated with a tremendous roar, lifting the *Tirpitz* 7ft out of the water and so damaging the ship that it never again ventured out into the open sea.

Cameron and Place were sent to Marlag-O prison camp for naval officers near Bremen and learned that they had both been awarded the Victoria Cross. One of their fellow prisoners was John Worsley, a talented artist, who painted both their portraits on a piece of bed sheet that had been used as scenery in camp theatricals. After the war, he became president of the Royal Society of Marine Artists.

Cameron, Donald, painting by John Worley.

Place, Godfrey, painting.

97

John Harman – Kohima VC

In the same way that Albert Ball was a lone wolf, so John Harman displayed the same traits. He was the first of five children born to Martin Harman, an entrepreneur who famously purchased the island of Lundy in the Bristol Channel. It was on Lundy that John Harman developed his love of nature and the freedom he experienced. John enlisted in the Army in November 1941 and joined the Household Cavalry but it became obvious from the start that military life did not suit him. Soon the Household Cavalry agreed with him

Harman Lundy Memorial.

and John joined a couple of regiments before being sent with the Royal Fusiliers to India. Just before Christmas 1943, he was transferred to the 4th Battalion, Royal West Kent Regiment, for the invasion of Burma. For three months, the regiment was continually engaged in the fighting and John appears to have relished this release from the daily drudgery he had endured for the past two years. They were sent north with the 5th Indian Division to the Naga Hills. A huge Japanese army was threatening to invade India by way of this remote region on the Burma–China border and the British rushed in all available forces to counter this threat. On 5 April 1944, the West Kents took up position at the vital road junction at Kohima. They arrived under fire from the surrounding hills and within a short time they were surrounded by the Japanese 31st Division. So began the epic Siege of Kohima.

John Harman.

The perimeter that the West Kents were defending was small and the Japanese had closed to within yards. The Japanese attack began in earnest on the night of the 6th and was repulsed. The next night, the Japanese had established a machine gun nest, which gave them a commanding field of fire. Harman crawled out of his position, slowly ran forward and, gathering momentum, he flung himself down at the very mouth of the bunker. He then took a four-second grenade, pulled the clip, counted to three and threw it through the slit. The two crewmen were killed and John returned with the machine gun.

On the 9th, five Japanese with machine guns and automatics were on a nearby ridge that overlooked the whole British position. John ordered a comrade on a Bren gun to give him covering fire as he dashed down the slope. Pausing, he aimed his rifle and shot one of the Japanese. He then moved on and shot another. By this time he was under automatic fire from the remaining three. Fixing his bayonet, John crossed the valley floor and dashed up the slope toward the Japanese position, ignoring the heavy incoming fire. By some miracle, he reached the post unscathed. Leaping down on the position, John bayoneted all three and held the machine gun up to the cheers of his comrades, before flinging it away amongst the trees. As he approached the safety of his own lines, a burst of machine gun fire hit him in his side, mortally wounding him. His father received his VC and had a memorial placed on Lundy.

98

John Brunt – Italian VC & MC

There cannot be many large villages that have a pub, a war memorial and a church with a large ornate stained glass window honouring the memory of their only Victoria Cross recipient; Paddock Wood in Kent has all three. John Brunt was born in Shropshire, the son of a farmer who sold up because of the recession and moved to Paddock Wood to manage a canning factory. John volunteered for the Army on leaving school in 1941, joining the local Royal West Kents. In 1943, he was commissioned in the Sherwood Foresters but was soon posted to the 6th Battalion, Royal Lincolnshire Regiment, and joined them in North Africa in time for the Tunis Campaign.

After taking part in some heavy fighting, the regiment joined the American Fifth Army under General Mark Clark in the Salerno landings, 50 miles south of Naples. Lieutenant John Brunt was involved with his platoon in much heavy fighting as they faced some of Germany's toughest fighting men. Gradually, the Fifth Army pushed its way from Salerno and on the night of 14/15 December 1943, John Brunt was awarded

Brunt VC window exterior 010.

the Military Cross for gallantry just north of the River Peccia, when his patrol attacked three houses occupied by the Germans. Armed with Tommy guns and grenades, the thirty-minute fight ended with eleven of the enemy dead and the houses captured. One member of the platoon had been seriously injured and Brunt carried him on his back, only for a surviving German to shoot the wounded man dead.

During the harsh Italian winter, the Lincolns had fought four hard battles and were rested in the Middle East before returning to Italy in July 1944. They were in time to take part in the attacks on the German Gothic Line, which was penetrated after some bitter fighting. Now they had to endure another dismal Italian winter with incessant cold rain that turned the ground into a muddy morass. In early December, the Lincolns suffered from the heavy shelling near Faenza and the foremost positions were relieved by the Carrier Platoon under the command of Captain John Brunt. Coincidentally, 6 December was his 22nd birthday, which was celebrated in a fierce three-day fight. On 9 December, the German 90 Panzer Grenadier Division, outnumbering Brunt's men three to one, launched an intense counter-attack. Taking up a Bren gun, Brunt accounted for fourteen of the enemy. With his radio destroyed, a runner brought a message to withdraw 200 yards and Brunt stayed behind to give covering fire for his platoon. When his Bren ammunition was exhausted, he grabbed a PIAT anti-tank launcher and a 2in mortar, which kept the Germans at a

Brunt, John.

distance. Later in the day, the Panzer Grenadiers resumed their attack. Brunt grabbed another Bren gun and rallied his men. Leaping onto a Sherman tank, he directed fire before jumping down and stalking the enemy with his Bren. In his VC citation it was noted that: 'Wherever the fighting was heaviest, Captain Brunt was always to be found moving from one post to another encouraging the men and firing any weapon he found at any target he could see.' Having coming through this fight unscathed, John Brunt was killed the next day by a stray mortar shell.

99

William Speakman – Korean War VC

One of the more controversial VCs of the 20th century was William Speakman. This was not because of his VC action on Hill 217 in Korea, which was exceptionally brave, but the way that untruths spread mostly by the press dogged his life. The general public believed that he had fought off the Chinese hordes with beer bottles and that he was a hellraiser. Despite his denials, the public preferred the more colourful version. Born in Altrincham, Cheshire, he joined the Black Watch, his stepfather's regiment, but served

Speakman, Bill, obverse of his VC. Scratched Hill 317.

Speakman greeted by Col. Carne VC.

most of his regimental life with the King's Own Scottish Borderers.

On 4 November 1951, the Chinese attacked a range of hills near the 38th Parallel. Private Bill Speakman collected six men and a pile of grenades and broke up the enemy's attacks, inflicting heavy casualties. In total, it was estimated that he threw 100 grenades and only stopped when they ran out. Resorting to hurling rocks, he enabled his company to withdraw.

In a 2003 interview with *The Times*, he recollected his VC action: 'We were out reinforcing the wire and had a funny feeling that something was going to happen. Two or three hours later all hell broke loose. There were thousands of Chinese; they must have concealed themselves like rabbits in the ground. They were very skilful at it. It was getting dark and we could only just pick them out. They came at us in a rush all along the front. There was a lot of hand to hand. There were three waves: the cannon fodder that flattened the wire, the second, and then the third are the really tough ones and you have to mix it with them. There were so many of them, you just had to get on with it.

'They were milling around you; you can't even pull your bolt back, so you fight with the butt of your rifle and bayonet. The battle went on for six hours; when we ran out of ammunition we started to throw rocks and stones and anything we could lay our hands on. I led up to 15 counter-charges; we had to get our wounded. We just couldn't give in; we'd fought so long we just couldn't give up that bloody hill. You are fighting for your life and it's your job to hold the line. If you give in they'll attack the other units from the rear.

'Fear? You are apprehensive, but you get used to it. You are looking right, left, behind you, watching out for anybody going under; you have to rescue them.

'I didn't know I had been singled out. There were other guys doing what I did, mates you knew you could rely on: if you looked behind, they were right behind you. They fought shoulder to shoulder, never let you down …

'A month later, on my way back to my unit, I was in a transit camp and the commandant sent for me. I hadn't a clue why; I thought they were going to say cherrio! I was marched in, there were two officers. "Are you Private Speakman, 14471590? I'm very proud to inform you that you have won the VC." The ribbon was pinned on my chest on parade in Korea. The medal had been awarded by the King and, after he died, presented to me by the Queen in Buckingham Palace. It was overwhelming.'

When Speakman sold his VC group, it was noticed that he had scratched 'Hill 217' on the reverse.

Speakman, William, VC.

100

Johnson Beharry – A Twice-Earned VC in Iraq

A poorly educated, dreadlocked pot-smoker from Grenada seems an unlikely VC hero. Told by a recruiting sergeant to go away and clean up his act, Beharry returned to become one of the British Army's best-known and respected soldiers. Afterwards he went to fulfil a public relations role with the Household Division and become a celebrity outside the military sphere.

After serving with the 1st Battalion, Princess of Wales's Royal Regiment (PWRR), in Kosovo and Northern Ireland, he was deployed in April 2004 to southern Iraq. Within two months, he was called upon to perform his acts of valour. In the early hours of 1 May, he was the driver of a Warrior armoured personnel carrier (APC) ordered to replenish an isolated outpost in Al-Amarah. This order changed to extracting a foot patrol that had become pinned down by a series of enemy ambushes. As they came to a roundabout, they saw the road ahead was empty, indicating a potential ambush area. Sure enough, they came under heavy fire, which rocked the Warrior and the platoon commander and gunner sustained wounds. Beharry realised that the best course was to drive through the ambush to

Beharry meets author in Madeira.

escape. He had to contend with a barricade that may have contained explosives but he safely drove through it. Seeing a rocket-propelled grenade (RPG) flying towards him, Beharry attempted to close the hatch but the RPG exploded near his head, damaging the hatch. A bullet penetrated his helmet but fortuitously lodged in the inner surface. Once he reached the British base, Cimic House, which was under fire, Beharry climbed onto the turret and pulled his wounded commander and gunner from the vehicle and got them to safety. Mounting his blazing APC, Beharry drove it into the Cimic House enclosure before collapsing from exhaustion.

Returning to duty after medical treatment, Beharry performed his second gallant action. On 11 June, his was the lead APC when it was

ambushed by RPGs. One detonated just 6in from Beharry's head, resulting in a serious head injury. Despite being blinded by the blood pouring from his wound, Beharry managed to reverse the Warrior out of the ambush and thus save his crew. The wound was life-threatening and he was evacuated to Selly Oak, Birmingham, where he lay in a coma. After a series of delicate operations, he made a recovery but his days as a serving soldier were over. On 27 April 2005, he received his Victoria Cross from the Queen, the first for forty years. Also present was the Chief of the General Staff, General Sir Mike Jackson, who declared; 'I can't remember feeling as proud of the Army as I do today.'

Johnson Beharry continued in the Army in a public relations capacity; signing books, attending memorial services, carrying the FA Cup at the final between Chelsea and Manchester United and taking part in an ice-skating dance competition on television. He was also tattooed with an image of the Victoria Cross, not discreetly on his arm, but one that covered his whole back.

Beharry, Damaged Helmet 1 May.

Beharry, Damaged Helmet 11 June.

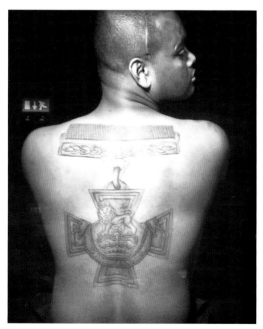

Beharry, J, tattoo.

Beharry, Madieram February 2007 026.